FROM SPINNING TO WINNING

SOLVING EARLY CAREER CONFUSION

TIM SULLIVAN

This book is dedicated to my dad as it is living proof of the completion of my own journey from my "spinning" love for him to a "winning" love of a son for his father. A long journey just completed.

CONTENTS

INTRODUCTION

There are a thousand ways to launch a career. Some of us rocket out of school and into a professional path we have been dreaming about since childhood. Most of us, myself included, stumble into one thing and then another, learning about our own strengths and wishes along the way. Certainly there are a lot of people whose experience falls somewhere between these extremes.

No matter which approach you take, though, there is a high probability you will eventually find yourself wondering whether you've gotten it all wrong. And really, *eventually* is likely to come sooner rather than later.

I know this because I see it all the time in my professional coaching practice. I meet younger people who thought the working world would be different. I see those who are on their second or third jobs – or occasionally, their third or fourth careers – and don't seem to be getting any closer to the right situation. I even come across senior executives, entrepreneurs, and other "high performers" who are entirely dissatisfied with the working portion of their lives.

The circumstances might vary, but the common denominator is that all these people have followed the same playbook. They've gotten the tried-and-true advice, just like you and I have, when it comes to finding a job and earning a living. Has it worked? To a certain degree we would have to admit it has. After all, most of us are gainfully employed. And yet we can *also* say the old tips and tricks failed spectacularly because a high percentage of men and women dread getting up in the morning.

After decades of watching this cycle play out from the outside *and* the inside, I have come to realize that there are some important steps missing in the traditional career planning process. To be more specific, there are some critical skills today's young people aren't being taught.

I have often heard the complaint that a person can't graduate high school without learning the Pythagorean theorem or the definition of biological RNA, even though that same person may not be able to change a flat tire or file their taxes after they have earned a diploma. I feel like a similar gap exists at the university level. There are plenty of clinics on writing a resume or surviving an entry-level job interview. However, there are very few resources that focus on tapping into your own passions, assessing your own marketability, or breaking out of the hamster wheel of traditional job search tactics.

I want to fill in the missing pieces. If you'd like to cut short decades of frustration before they begin, then this is the book you didn't realize you needed.

In the coming chapters we are going to have a lot of fun. I'm going to share some fun stories and analogies. Stick with me and you will learn all about uncharted rivers in undiscovered lands, job search marbles that you can trade for a brighter future, and even an obscure desert healer who has all of life's most elusive answers. Along the way you're also going to learn why managing your career requires a business mindset, the best way to find current and future opportunities, and why your next job might not even exist yet.

Doesn't that sound like more fun than tinkering with the objective line on your resume for the hundredth time? This adventure won't just be more interesting, but it will also be a lot more productive.

Before we jump in, though, I want to share a few thoughts about who this book is for and how you can get the most value from it.

The target audience for this book is the recent graduate who is facing turmoil in their career. That means that as we go, I'm going to assume you are in your mid- to late 20s, or possibly early 30s, and have had one or two jobs already. You may be discovering for the first time that your career plan isn't as complete as you thought it was, or that you are facing challenges you didn't expect.

Most of the same lessons and ideas will apply to new or upcoming graduates. If you have recently left school, or plan to in the coming months, then you might not yet have any professional experience that extends beyond internships and part-time jobs. That's no problem. What I have to teach can help you avoid the mistakes your friends and peers have been making.

And finally, I want to acknowledge that some readers might be in a different stage of their career paths. Perhaps you bought this book for someone else and are giving it a look. Maybe you are in your 40s or 50s and feel like you need to make a change, or that you're still figuring things out. You can still get value from the coming exercises and ideas as well, although you might be better suited for my next book, which will focus on solving mid-career challenges. That book is designed for those of us who are farther along in our careers.

No matter which group you belong to, though, the main obstacles toward fulfillment are the same. And the advice I have to give is every bit as helpful. Keep reading. Follow the exercises. And then buy a copy for some other young professional in your life. Better yet, buy dozens of them for *all* the new and recent graduates you know. They will thank you later, and so will I.

Most of the people I work with in my coaching practice aren't fresh out of school. I mainly deal with executives and leaders. But I wanted to aim this book at the younger crowd because you are most open to advice while simultaneously needing it most. As new competitors in the job market, you are in a position to set yourselves off in the right direction before wasting years or decades on the wrong path.

So, if you feel like your professional journey hasn't started the way you hoped it would, then know you're in the right place. If you haven't even graduated yet, keep reading and take the lessons I have to share on board. And if you're a bit farther down the road, then follow along and adapt your approach as needed.

Let's not get hung up on the details, though. Whoever you are, wherever you are, and whatever your current career path looks like, I want to help. If you are frustrated with your current job, or the career track you have found yourself on, then it's time to start looking at things differently.

I have structured this book in a way that (hopefully) makes it feel like a series of one-on-one coaching sessions that just happen to be taking place through print. The only requirements are that you keep an open mind, have a bit of fun, and fill in your parts of the conversation when I ask you to. After all, I can give the advice but you still have to make the decisions and follow through.

That's actually good news, because this is all about your life and career. Let's work together to make them everything you have dreamed of.

1

READY TO TAKE THE LEAP?

Not long ago, a colleague of mine forwarded me an article outlining all the reasons it's a difficult time to be starting a career. It laid out half a dozen unprecedented challenges recent graduates face, ranging from a pandemic to a changing economy and the uncertainties associated with automation. The authors went on to explain that technologies like artificial intelligence would change some industries in ways that were impossible to predict, making it difficult to even imagine a future that extended beyond the next decade.

The thing about this article is that I've seen hundreds like it. They come out every year. And they are *always* on target.

Young people face strong headwinds when venturing out into the real world in every era. The conditions are rarely, if ever, ideal for someone who is getting their start. There are wars, recessions, technology-related upheavals, and societal changes that take place within every generation. It's a never-ending cycle of destruction and opportunity.

My point? If you're reading this you've got it hard. But so did almost everyone else who was once in your shoes. That doesn't mean it's hopeless. You can find your way to the right job, the right path, and even a life that makes you engaged and fulfilled. You just have to know what you're up against and how to make good choices.

That's what this book is all about.

Whether you're holding a tablet, an e-reader, or an old-fashioned set of bound paper pages, you aren't getting the standard set of career and job search advice. I wouldn't do that to you because a lot of what you hear about finding a job simply isn't rooted in reality. Instead, I'm going to give you some real insights from a life and career that has had a bit of everything – big promotions and large bonuses, periods of poverty and aimlessness, some entrepreneurial success, and a dash of business partner thievery.

I've done many of the things you might dream of, like winning awards and starting a company. I've also gone broke, found myself stuck in a dead-end job, and had to reinvent my career at a few points. Eventually, I ended up as a hybrid career and life coach. That has put me in a spot to share not only my own wins and losses, but also stories and perspectives from hundreds of others.

I'm packaging all of this into the book you're reading for one simple reason: I don't want you to be overwhelmed the way so many of my peers and clients have been. The path to the life you're looking for is hardly ever smooth, but neither is your preferred destination impossibly far away. I want to take some of the twists and bumps out of the road for you. Follow me and I'll take you to a place where you're more focused, more fulfilled, and less likely to make the huge mistakes that can keep you stuck at the career plan starting line or, even worse, locked into a job or role that fills you with dread and boredom.

My Career Coaching Philosophy

When you're facing challenge or change in any part of your life, there are essentially two things that need to happen: first, you have to figure out what you want. Then, you need to work out a way to make it a reality. The average human struggles with both parts of that plan, usually because emotion gets in the way. That's why you are likely to feel overwhelmed when considering career options. Luckily, you have a new friend and coach (your friendly author, Timbo) who can show you the way.

At various points in my career I've been an award-winning salesperson, a classics teacher and hockey coach, and a professional consultant (which is just a different kind of coaching for businesses). I hope you'll recognize right away that this means I've had to change careers myself on a couple of occasions... usually after figuring out my current plan wouldn't work. More importantly, I want you to know how those different experiences influenced my methods and how those methods can help you.

As a salesperson, I learned early on that it was important to know all about your products and the best ways to present them to potential customers. As a coach, I saw that systems and models were invaluable for turning abstract concepts into actionable plans. And as a teacher, I quickly recognized that no one learns anything when they are bored.

Those three insights have helped me enormously throughout my career. In this book I want to combine them. That means we are going to start with a different way of thinking about you that puts the "product" front and center while we come up with a business plan for the next few years. As part of that we are going to break down big ideas into simple, interactive exercises that lead you to lots of little epiphanies. Best of all, we're going to do all of this without resorting to textbook-style quizzes and diagrams. Instead we are going to use exercises, stories, and occasionally jokes.

That might make this a much different kind of job search or career guide than the ones you are used to looking at. That's all right. I chose this format for the book for a couple of reasons. The first is that it's consistent with my personal style. I don't want to try to be something I'm not, and I don't want you to pretend either.

The second reason has to do with organization and actionability. I tend to be a big-picture kind of person. I like large projects and sweeping concepts. I don't do as well with details and minutia. That can lead me down some interesting paths, but it can also cause me to leave projects half-finished.

As an example, this book started as a set of presentations for graduating college seniors more than 20 years ago. Although I kept giving the talks every year, and recording some thoughts along the way, the manuscript never really seemed to come together. To actually do something with all the knowledge I had been accumulating I needed to slice the outlines, letters, and diagrams I was holding on to down into simpler pieces.

It's often the same with our own lives and careers. We can get overwhelmed in dozens of different ways, but no matter how far down we get, time never stops. Life keeps moving and there are new avenues to explore and decisions to make. That makes it incredibly difficult for any of us to catch our breath, much less gain perspective.

By sorting the most important things I've learned into little vignettes and activities I've made them into something you can follow along without getting too deep into the weeds. The information might seem like a lot at certain points, but I'm hoping you'll stick with me and just keep moving from one chapter exercise to the next. Sometimes you just have to follow along in context before the pieces make sense.

I have worked as a highly paid coach and consultant to develop the same kinds of processes for international companies, and have walked high-performing executives through some of the same exact routines. One thing I've never been able to do, though, is create change for someone else through my words or activity alone. The processes I am going to share *will* work but you're going to have to put in a bit of effort to see the benefit. This isn't the kind of book you can just read and put away.

With that in mind, I can promise you once more that our time together isn't going to be exhausting the way some career planning guides are. In fact, I'm going to bet that the farther you go through this process the better and lighter you're going to feel. That's because you'll gain confidence and a sense of purpose. Your future is unfolding in front of you one second at a time. You can't stop change from coming, but you *can* direct it in a way that puts the life you want firmly within reach.

If we can agree on that goal, and that we should have some fun along the way, then you're ready to get started. The first thing to do is change the way you think about yourself with respect to employers. Before we can get to all of that, though, you should probably know just a little bit about who I am and why you should listen to me. So, let's get the introductions out of the way.

2

THE TALE OF TIMBO

"What can you tell me about yourself?" ranks as one of the all-time most-hated interview questions. It's incredibly difficult to condense decades of life and experience into a short and compelling narrative that will interest another person... much less get them to hire you.

I'm reminded of that now as I look to explain the highlights and lowlights of a long career in a few pages. I've probably been living three times as long as the average reader of this book. Reducing it all to a couple dozen paragraphs while trying to explain my usefulness to you isn't easy. I'm going to give it a try, though, and I hope you'll bear with me. By the end of this chapter you'll have a quick sense of who I am, where my perspectives on career planning come from, and why I can help you.

I'll start by saying I come from Boston. My family represents the classic story of middle-class immigrant success. My grandfather was a peat farmer in Ireland. For those who don't know, it's probably a rung below "barnacle scraper" on the career ladder. But my grandfather wasn't the oldest son on the farm, so he didn't inherit the family's plot of land. Seeking fame and fortune (or maybe just enough to eat at the end of each day), he set off for America like so many others did back in the early 1900s.

Grampa Tim ended up in West Haven, Connecticut. He married a woman he had never met before, my Gramma Tess, whose family lived less than a mile from the Sullivan farm on the Ring of Kerry in Ireland. The story, as Ma told me, was that Tess had Grampa Tim work the night shift as a trolley car driver so that she could raise their three children "her way." I guess romance hadn't been invented yet. Dad was raised with a devoted mother, two sisters, and a mostly absent father. He soldiered on and did what any good immigrant's child was supposed to: studied hard and got into Yale.

During his college days he married his younger sister's best friend. Together he and my mother raised six children: four girls, myself, and my younger brother, Michael. I had a fun childhood. I got into scrapes and bits of trouble, like kids do, but kept up my grades. I also found a bit of talent for my favorite sport, hockey. All in all, life was pretty good.

The expectation was that I would follow in my father's footsteps and go to Yale. However, during a visit with a friend to Bowdoin College in Maine, I fell in love with the campus and met the hockey coach I wanted to play for. I begged the admissions board to let me apply at the last minute and they relented. I think my dad would have preferred I went to Yale, but I loved Bowdoin so he didn't put up a huge fight. Over time he even came to love my alma mater as well.

I'm sure I don't have to tell you how strange it was to make the transition to college life. The freedom was so foreign and exciting to me. After twelve years of dealing with Catholic nuns in elementary school and priests in high school, Bowdoin seemed like a free-for-all. Freshman year was both a ball and a disaster! Despite having pulled in high grades throughout high school I started college by taking all the wrong classes, losing my confidence, partying heavily, and nearly flunking out. I stayed on, though, and found my stride. Like my mother and four sisters, I ended up pursuing my love of the classics and majored in Latin. I secured spots on the varsity hockey and golf teams.

School and sports kept me busy, but apparently not busy enough. Before long I started a serious relationship with a lovely young woman named Joan and got married early in my junior year. Life was suddenly the same and yet very different all at once. I kept going to class and hockey season was still underway. But with a year and a half of college remaining to complete and a baby on the way, it was time to think ahead.

Teaching and coaching became my career focus. It made sense on a lot of different levels. I wanted to help people, which I could certainly do as a sculptor of young minds. Being a teacher meant I could continue to stay involved with hockey and golf, which was alluring. And, teaching also meant avoiding the war in Vietnam. Grading papers seemed like a better option than dodging bullets.

The issue for those of us graduating at that time was that there were no jobs. No one was hiring. A trip to the local library revealed that there were exactly five schools on the East Coast that met my criteria of having a hockey team and being less than a mile from the ocean. I decided to visit the first one in person. By just showing up I was able to convince both the hockey coach and classics teacher that each could hire me half time! (Note to job seekers: this type of job creation CAN happen for you!)

Two years into this wonderful position, it became apparent that I should earn a master's degree. The headmaster promised me a position when I returned and off I went to UMass Amherst to spend a year earning a master's degree and serving as a teaching assistant to get the credentials I needed. This is when the next challenge in my young life occurred: my perfect job at the first school had been given away. In spite of what the headmaster said, he had filled the position (with a good friend of mine, no less.)

Fortunately, I was able to land a second teaching position in northern New England. I loved working with the headmaster, and he enjoyed mentoring me as well. In fact, he wanted me to be the earmarked successor for his job, giving me the life and security I had been looking for. What more could I ask for? My daughter Lisa was healthy, and my wife had just given birth to our second girl, Kelly, and a third was on the way. Now I was slated to take over a respected position with unmatched job security.

His offer should have made me jump up and down with joy. *A headmaster before the age of 30? Yes! But then also NO!*

Even with two baby girls at home and my dear son "in the oven," I somehow knew I had to give up my steady paycheck. Prep school teaching and administration were no longer my goals. I had a hard time understanding my own gut emotions. There was a push and pull inside of me that was impossible to explain. No one else could feel them, but to me they were every bit as real as a hard fall on the ice. The best way to describe it would be the unmistakable feelings of being isolated and trapped.

I knew what my logical mind told me, but I also couldn't deny the truth inside. The money from my teaching job was meager but there would be plenty in time. Finances weren't the trouble. It was the potential monotony of decades to come that was frightening to me. I was cloistered. Stuck.

Deep down I knew something I couldn't quite express, so I decided to make a decision that felt bold to me and downright reckless to my wife. I was going to change careers. Luckily, I had a direction in mind. I had recently met a Northwestern Mutual life insurance agent who happened to be visiting a teacher at my school. The agent recruited me and I traveled an hour away to visit at his office in western Massachusetts. The high quality of the Northwestern Mutual appealed to me greatly. It felt like a larger Bowdoin, an established firm with rock-solid midwestern values.

Moving into a straight commission job wasn't exactly ideal for the circumstances my wife and I were in, but I was more afraid of the life I would lead if I remained where I was than I was of going broke. I could not say the same for Joan. Things were tough at home.

Even so, life in Greenfield, MA, was good to us. My son, JT Sullivan III, was born there. I was the hockey coach for our local high school's varsity team and quickly became a success in my new career.

As it turned out, I had a real talent for selling insurance policies. It allowed me to do the thing I love most – help people – while also showing off my competitive side. And, as someone who finds happiness in human-to-human contact, the job brought lots of interesting challenges and interactions.

A few years went by and I wasn't just selling insurance policies; I was selling *a lot* of them. I won local and then national awards. (As an aside, the exceptional training I received from Northwestern in "consultative selling" techniques have become the foundation of what I will teach you later in the book when you are ready to find the job you want.)

I wasn't sure I actually enjoyed my work, but I started making some real money and so I assumed I should just keep my head down and appreciate the fact that I was doing well. Besides, a lot of things felt right. I loved the freedom, the relationships that were being formed, and the fact that I had a bright future. Getting paychecks that were several times what I'd earned as a teacher didn't hurt, either.

Still, there were cracks forming below the surface. As a high-performing salesman I was tapped for a move into management. Making the move would have entailed a few years in Milwaukee for training, followed by a move to *Anywhere, USA,* for a permanent posting. Joan had already followed me through one career and location change; she put her foot down when I brought up the idea of making another. She was too attached to New England and I wasn't willing to push an ultimatum.

To be fair, I'm not completely sure I would have taken the promotion even if she had agreed. I think I would have been good at the job, but would I have enjoyed it?

I guess I'll never know. What I *can* say is the nagging feeling that life insurance wasn't right for me wouldn't go away. My career was still trending upward, but my mood didn't follow. After five years we made a short move to Boston where I had an opportunity to keep selling while also managing a half dozen other new sales recruits. The '70s were turning into the '80s and the world was changing. So was my life.

This was the decade when I discovered my true calling. It was also a period of time that nearly broke me mentally and emotionally.

I transitioned away from my insurance sales position and into a role as a career development advisor (how's that for irony?) thanks to a referral from a high school friend. He knew I was looking for something new and introduced me to the head of the Boston office of Arthur Andersen & Co., which at the time was one of the world's biggest accounting firms.

How was I able to make that sort of move without any previous coaching and consulting experience? Don't worry, we are going to get to the specific steps and details you need to follow in the coming chapters. What I want you to understand for the moment is that this was probably the greatest and most fortunate event in my professional life. It helped me finally turn my passions into a viable career. And, it just so happened to have occurred at a point when my life seemed to be devolving into chaos around me. My brother-in-law, brother, father and close friend of my father all passed away suddenly within 24 months. This all occurred while my marriage was dissolving before my very eyes.

I hope you'll never go through these same things, but I want to warn you that you will go through *something*. You are undoubtedly going to face moments of turmoil and uncertainty. No amount of planning, and no perfectly written career guide, can stop that from happening. What I want you to remember is that these times can lead to sleepless nights, but also to breakthroughs that push you in directions you didn't even know existed.

Ultimately, the decade I spent consulting for Arthur Andersen helped me develop into the truest and best version of myself. It was there that I found my passion for helping others grow. Looking back, it seems clear to me that I unknowingly served as my own first client.

Eventually I outgrew my role at Arthur Andersen and decided to get entrepreneurial. It took some fits and starts, but eventually I ended up founding my firm, Wellesley Partners, with my wonderful second (and final) wife, Maryann. For many years I have helped job seekers and executives solve all kinds of crazy problems. Even though life and work can seem chaotic from one day to the next, it's a business and career that suit me perfectly.

There is more to my story, but you are probably picking up on the important themes. But just in case you missed any of them, understand that I've been in your shoes. I know what it's like to be scared, overwhelmed, and uncertain. I also know how to get through those situations, because I've done it myself and coached hundreds of others through them, too. And finally, I don't take any of this (or myself) too seriously. If you can remember that life is funny and that shit is bound to happen, you'll have a much easier time with the process we're about to go through together... not to mention the next four or five decades of your life.

3

WELCOME TO MYCO

One of the greatest things about coaching is that it gives you the gift of perspective.

After living through my own early career turmoil, I had the chance to work with some 20-something superstar accountants at Arthur Andersen in the '80s. What I learned was that these bright and ambitious young professionals were all suffering from the same issues I had grappled with. However, they were processing them in a different way.

For instance, all of them were working long days. In fact, I would say they were putting in way too many hours for their own good. Because they were being assigned detailed tasks – a.k.a. "grunt work" – that kept them busy through evenings and weekends, they had no social lives whatsoever. This led them to feeling disillusioned.

When they weren't being sent to make copies or run errands, they were being trained in corporate evaluation and the fundamentals of business modeling. They could meet a new client, carefully study numerical data and historical trends, and then understand the challenges an organization was facing. They could perform these deep dives quickly and thoroughly, ultimately coming to not only the problems entrepreneurs and executives were facing, but also the solutions our firm could provide for those issues.

This was ironic because they were absolutely clueless when it came to understanding themselves, their own motivations, or their skills. In other words, they couldn't turn their analytical minds inward. These were smart young people, nearly every one of them arriving at the company with a 4.0 GPA from a great school. And yet, they were just as lost and stuck as everyone else.

In the process of working with these brilliant but confused gems an idea came to me: given that they were so good at evaluating businesses, why not have them use the same tools to think about their own careers? Given that they were confident in this one area, couldn't they apply the same process to a different set of skills?

With that, the *MyCo* model was born. Over time, I've learned that it's not just useful for young analysts but anyone who needs to sort out their own career path.

A Consultant's Approach to a Psychologist's Problem

Let's go back to the situation I described a couple of paragraphs ago: the feeling of working hard and being lost. It's the frustrating reality these young people were facing, and one I had stumbled through in my own life. It probably feels familiar to you, as well, which is why you picked this book up.

If we were to stop thinking about this as a personal or emotional experience and consider it rationally as a business challenge, how would things change? That's what I asked myself several decades ago. Here is what I found, as presented to these 20-somethings one-on-one:

- Your career is one of the most important parts of your life.
- However, you're trying to run that career with no data or historical information. I.e., you don't know who you are, what you're good at, or where you're trying to go.
- The little bit of data you do have lives in your head. It swims around up there and changes as frequently as the tides change daily.
- With no data, no direction, and no control over your focus you have no plan. As they say, failing to plan is planning to fail. Without any plan you have no control of your future. And with no control of your future you are, by definition, *out of control.*
- *Ergo, you are screwed.*

This is a very big problem. But most business problems have solutions, and this one is no different. I thought back to my sales and marketing training for Northwestern Mutual. One of the first things I learned as an agent was that you needed a personal business plan to stay successful (in that case, wealthy and employed).

To develop this plan you had to understand your product, including its strengths and weaknesses. You also had to position that product the right way for customers and clients. And finally, you needed to develop a campaign that didn't just help you find clients, but to do so in a way that flowed naturally from what you knew about your products and your market.

I realized the young CPAs at Arthur Andersen were lacking the same kind of process and perspective. In order to help them break out of the ruts they were in I needed them to do three things:

#1 Gain a Bit of Product Knowledge

Who are you, *really*? What are your strengths and weaknesses? What would your friends, employers, and professors say about you? Would they call you funny, comical, musical, introverted, cautious, caring, driven, aloof, or intuitive (as examples)? Would they say you are competitive, or have a need for control?

The average young person needs to be asking themselves a lot of questions along these lines.

#2 Position Yourself in the Market

What do you want? You should try to describe your definition of the ideal job. How do your dreams, wants, and desires fit in with the list of qualities you identified about yourself?

As a quick aside, a lot of young people I work with are really blown away by the logic of those first two steps. The truth is most of us skip these when looking for a job and the results are usually horrific. There's lots of activity with no results. Or worse, we find ourselves in a role that doesn't fit us at all.

#3 Develop a Sales Campaign

Your job search campaign should give you a step-by-step plan you can follow to find the right position. Just as important, though, is that it be tied to the first two steps. In other words, the job you get needs to fit who you are and what you want. Otherwise you'll be banging your head against the wall in no time.

When you take a step back from the frustration you feel and think about things this way, it gets easier to evaluate your situation based on facts. More importantly, it allows you to develop a plan of action.

For that reason, I asked the young people I was coaching to think of themselves as the CEO of a new company called *My Corporation*, or *MyCo* for short. It's the same challenge I'm going to give you.

As the chief executive you are in total control. You also happen to be the only salesperson and the product the company sells all at the same time. That's a lot of moving parts, but you are in charge of all of them.

Of course, those young Arthur Andersen CPAs didn't feel like they were in control of anything. Soon, though, after embracing this model and completing the exercises I'm going to outline in the coming chapters, they realized they were only pretending to be helpless victims. Once they figured out they had the privilege and responsibility of deciding where their lives would go, things began to change immediately.

Why You Should Think of Yourself Like a Company

I have presented the *MyCo* framework to hundreds of people over the years. The most common response is "I never thought about my career that way." That's what makes the idea so valuable. It can offer a fresh perspective on a common problem.

You shouldn't just take my word for it, though. Let's take a brief look at how the habit of thinking of yourself as the CEO of your own life and career can change things dramatically.

You might think to yourself that you didn't study business in school, or that you aren't the kind of person who looks at spreadsheets and investment reports for fun. In that case, it might seem as if the *MyCo* model isn't that valuable. I would strongly disagree. There are a lot of benefits that come to following along with this thought exercise.

The first benefit has to do with perspective. One of the reasons it's so easy to get into a funk, and stay there, has to do with the limited point of view we all have when it comes to self-evaluation. When you are down, stressed, or depressed, all you see are the problems sitting right in front of you. Everything you want lies on the other side of a seemingly immovable object.

That is not likely to be an accurate picture of your situation. The reality is there are almost always dozens (or more) potential solutions to the issues we face. However, that doesn't stop us from feeling stifled or frustrated. Because we are used to looking at things a certain way, and solving problems with certain tools or processes, we fail to consider different viewpoints. As the old saying goes, when all you have is a hammer, every problem looks like a nail.

By going through the process of imagining yourself as a stand-alone business you change the conversation in your mind. You ask yourself new questions and think in a way that is more rooted in facts than emotions. Sometimes, that can be enough to break the deadlock in your mind all by itself.

A person who is struggling to find a job, or to escape a situation that feels helpless, can get trapped in a line of thinking that reaches emotional dead ends. It's easy to get bogged down in feeling "not good enough." But an executive with a growth plan doesn't have the luxury of dwelling on self-pity.

The emotional new graduate might want to sit in their pajamas all day and watch cartoons if they haven't gotten any responses to their resume submissions. The chief executive isn't looking for excuses or asking for days off. That person is tasked with growing the company and they are willing to work nights and weekends to reach their goals.

Another reason to think like a CEO is that it engages the parts of your mind that involve strategy and long-term planning. They put themselves in charge of meeting revenue goals. They know that doing so will involve making investments, hiring others, working with consultants, and jumping into difficult decisions. In other words, they start problem solving... which can be the hardest thing to do when you're focused on your own misery.

Business leaders are driven by logic and data, something most new graduates and job seekers are short on. You can't make good decisions without the right information. I think it's fair to say most people, regardless of their age or career history, will spend more time planning a weekend trip than they will the next five years of their working life. That's a minor tragedy, and it can lead you to a lot of mistakes that would have been avoidable with a bit of foresight.

This actually brings us to the biggest benefit of all, and the natural conclusion from these other points: thinking about *MyCo* puts you in control.

No successful business ever had a plan that involved "calling a few customers and seeing how things turn out." Instead, profitable companies devise detailed strategies with budgets, schedules, and even contingency plans. Their leaders think about what is going to happen next week, next quarter, and next year. Once they are established in the market they start thinking decades ahead. They know conditions on the ground will change and evolve constantly, but that doesn't prevent them from moving forward with a big-picture plan that guides them toward a specific outcome.

You already understand that most of the people you know have never thought about their own careers in these terms. What I want you to consider now are the implications. How can any of us reach our goals if those targets aren't spelled out? How likely are we to get ahead, or feel fulfilled, if we never take time to write down the things that actually matter?

Your career, and your life as a whole, should be lived in an intentional way. I want you to be something that happens to the workforce, not to have your career be something that happens to you. The whole idea behind *MyCo* is that it stops you from doing things the way everyone else does and puts you on a path that you've actually chosen.

Most of us lease our lives and our time, again and again, instead of owning the present and the future. I want you to be the CEO of *MyCo* and the chief executive of your own life and destiny. That won't happen by accident, so it's time to fill in some of the details in your plan.

4

BUILDING YOUR PERSONAL BUSINESS

I t doesn't matter what *MyCo* looks like right now. What matters is where it is headed. You might be at the bottom of the career ladder at the moment, but who cares? Companies like Microsoft and Amazon were founded in garages and spare rooms. You have plenty of time to grow.

The one thing that will determine your success or failure in the future is your ability to be intentional about your next moves. If you were actually starting a corporation you would meet with a CPA, draw up some paperwork, open a business bank account, and maybe locate a small office space. The business I want you to think about is conceptual, so you don't need any of these things. However, you should develop some initial plans and ideas.

What Is Your Business All About?

Imagine for a second that you were starting your own company in the real world rather than an imaginary one in your mind. What would it sell?

You don't have to be constrained by reality when finding an answer. For example, you could make space ships even if you have no background in physics or engineering. Or, you could book musical acts for appearances all over the world despite the fact that you don't have any connections in that business. Just daydream for a minute or two about having a business and think about the way it would generate revenue.

Whatever came to you, think about what that business would give you personally. Would it be money? Security? The chance to experience more travel and adventure? Your own answers might be similar or completely different.

Over the next several chapters I'm going to walk you through lots of little exercises just like this one, designed to uncover your deepest dreams and values. For now I just want you to remember that your personal business is all about you. That sounds obvious, but it means that your dreams are yours alone. Maybe you want to be rich and influential. Perhaps you want more free time. It could be that you value family more than anything else.

The point of *MyCo* isn't to maximize profits unless that happens to be your goal. Instead, it's all about delivering the life and career you want. Sometimes clients lose sight of that in all the business-related analogies. While I'm going to ask you to think critically and analytically about yourself as we work through this model, that doesn't mean you actually have to prioritize business and finances within your own life.

With that being said, there are a couple of business-related tasks facing you as the new CEO of *MyCo*. The first is to get some outside advice.

Forming Your Board of Directors

In a corporation, the chief executive officer (or CEO) is the ultimate decision-maker. He or she sets the tone, devises a strategy, and is tasked with seeing the business through to its goals. It's not an easy job, but that's why this person gets the big office and the fat paycheck.

Although the CEO might ultimately be responsible for results, they don't have to make decisions alone. They typically have a team of advisors who can offer other perspectives. These individuals sit on a Board of Directors.

In the world of business, board members can be chosen on the basis of experience, technical expertise, or even familial connections. A board member could be a successful executive who retired from the same company or another well-known organization. They could be a professor, an author, or even a former politician. Or a board member could be someone from the founder's family if the company began as a smaller operation.

These are only examples, but they get to a bigger point: a Board of Directors should be made up of individuals who all know something about the company *and* have a vested interest in seeing it succeed. For reasons that might be personal or financial, they advise the CEO on big decisions.

As the brand-new CEO of *MyCo* it is incredibly important that you have the support you need from others, and particularly those who have the kinds of experience and connections that you don't. Not only can they serve as a sounding board for your biggest ideas, but they can also use their knowledge and connections to help you bring your plans to life.

It's often the case that our worst decisions are made in a vacuum. We get trapped in our own swirling thoughts, positive or negative, without seeing outside considerations or long-term consequences.

How many times have you looked back on a decision in your life and wondered how much differently things could have turned out if only someone who knew a bit more had filled you in on the risks or opportunities? How many times would you have liked to steer a sibling or friend in the right direction before they did something stupid?

This is what your personal Board of Directors is all about. They are going to encourage your best ideas and steer you away from the decisions that aren't likely to pan out in your favor.

Who belongs on this board? There aren't any hard and fast rules. For most of us, parents and family members are going to represent an obvious starting point. If you have someone in your life that you know and respect, add them to your list of candidates. It isn't necessarily important they have much (or any) knowledge in your field or work. What matters more is that they know you.

On the other side of the spectrum, you might consider professors and professional contacts. These people may not know you as well as your family does, but they should have some idea of your skills, personality, and ambitions. Also, they have the benefit of being able to see you as an up-and-coming CEO rather than someone whose diapers they used to change. Think about the classes you have taken, the jobs you have held, and any internships you might have completed. Whom have you met that you could turn to for the occasional cup of coffee with a side of advice or perspective?

In some cases, friends or colleagues could serve on your board. They may lack experience, as you do, but contribute a different point of view. If nothing else, they can help you compare notes and hold you accountable to your own goals and promises.

And finally, don't rule out others in your extended network, or just beyond. It may be that a local business owner whom you admire would be open to meeting with you now and then. Or, that a person who has found success in your intended industry would agree to serve as a mentor.

Ideally, you will have some sort of mix of each of these roles as types within your Board of Directors. After all, you want to hear different voices. You don't gain anything when everyone agrees with you, or even with each other. You need to think about things that wouldn't occur to you, or points of view that would otherwise be hidden. That's how your board is going to help you spot opportunities and avoid big blunders.

Note that you don't have to treat your personal Board of Directors as a formal entity. You might not ever use that terminology with them, and you don't have to meet with them all at once. Neither do you have to solicit their advice regularly. In fact, most people I work with talk to board members quite a bit at the beginning of the process I'm about to teach you (for reasons you will soon understand). But after they find themselves established in a new role, they may touch base a lot less frequently – maybe once every two or three years. In that time some board members may come and go.

As with most of the ideas in this book, the exact number of board members you have, and their specific identities, isn't important. What *is* important is the realization that you are responsible for creating the right results for *MyCo*. The key decisions, along with the credit or blame for them, will always come down to you. But you don't have to figure out everything on your own all the time. It might be your business, but it isn't a solo venture.

Creating a *MyCo* Business Plan

Once you understand the concept of your career as a company, the need to start planning and organizing information becomes very clear. In the coming chapters, I'm going to help you fill in the blanks in your strategic plan. By the time we're done, you'll know a lot more about yourself and the hiring process than you did when we started. You will also have a huge leg up on the millions of others out there who are trying to jumpstart their careers without the same sort of insights.

We will begin by brushing up your product knowledge. What does *MyCo* actually sell? To put this another way, what do you bring to the table as a professional?

You probably have more to offer employers than you might think. New and recent graduates often make the mistake of thinking they aren't qualified to do anything more complex than grabbing coffee. Meanwhile they may have certain skills from internships and life experiences that even seasoned industry veterans don't. I'm going to help you figure out where your most marketable qualities lie, and to use them in a way that aligns with your talents and wishes. No more settling for the first entry-level job offer that comes around.

Next, we will move on to your sales and marketing plan. This is where you package that fantastic product (you) and share with the customers who need it most (employers). If taking action without understanding your own strengths and plans is the most common career mistake, then looking for a job without considering basic sales principles comes in a close second.

You have probably taken years' worth of courses in chemistry and geometry to get to this point in your life. And yet, you might not have the faintest idea of what it takes to get your resume noticed by an employer. Isn't that a bit odd? My point is that even though academic knowledge is important, so too are business basics. It won't matter how qualified or energetic you are if recruiters and employers can't find out about you. We will make sure they do.

And finally, we are going to combine everything you learn about yourself, the job market, and the businesses you want to work for into an actionable plan that carries you through the next few years. As with all plans, ours is going to be flexible. No one can know what the future holds, and the life you have five years from now might look completely different from the one you are expecting to live today. That's the beauty of existing on planet Earth.

The point of having a great business plan is to lead yourself in the right direction, not necessarily to reach a certain destination. Our dreams tend to be moving targets. The career I have today suits me perfectly, but it's one I wouldn't have even been able to imagine when I was in my 20s. Your ideal path might not even exist yet. Maybe it's out there waiting for you to invent it.

Are you ready to dive in? Let's begin by learning more about the wonderful, one-of-a-kind product you have to sell to the world.

5

YOU CAN'T SELL WHAT YOU DON'T UNDERSTAND

W hen I made my first major career transition it was from academia to sales. I hadn't made much money as a teacher, but at least it was a steady paycheck. Moving into a straight commission role felt like a huge gamble, particularly with an anxious wife and two young children at home.

Making matters worse was the fact that my graduate degree in Latin didn't exactly prepare me for a job selling life insurance. Actually, it didn't really prepare me for *anything* except to bore young people with the intricacies of a dead language. Still, I think you can see what I'm getting at.

Before I could master selling, or learn about details like contracts and negotiations, I had to understand the basics. That meant learning about the different kinds of insurance policies on the market, and specifically the ones my company could offer. How could I hope to gain a single new client – much less earn the kinds of commissions it would take to feed my growing family – if I didn't even know what my company had for people to buy?

You can't sell what you don't know or understand. It might seem obvious, but this simple fact is something people miss again and again. It's true for a person who needs to earn commission from the sales of products and services. It's *also* true for a new graduate or young professional who is trying to sell themselves to an employer. If you don't know who you are, what you bring to the table, or where you're trying to go, then you don't have a whole lot to offer. You need to be selling something other than a blank slate.

This is why product knowledge – a.k.a. understanding your own strengths and weaknesses – is so important.

Of course, even if you *can* identify your own talents and skills, you still have to decide what you want to do with them. The answers might not be as obvious as you think. As I've already pointed out, most people operate under the mistaken assumption that they should already know exactly what they want and how to get it. That's because the message out there in the world, and particularly on social media, is that everyone else is focused and goal driven. Dig deeper and you'll see that is rarely the case. Even phenomenally successful individuals are often figuring things out as they go along. They are constantly adjusting their plans and ideas.

What I'm trying to tell you is that it's all right if you don't know what you can give to employers, or even what you truly want to be doing in the first place. And even if you feel certain you know who you are and where your career is headed, I hope you'll stick with me over the next couple of chapters. Be willing to explore your own answers and challenge your assumptions. You might be surprised at what you will learn.

The better you know and understand yourself the easier it gets to land on a career path that is going to bring you wealth, fulfillment, or anything else you might happen to be after. The more I knew about insurance, the easier it was to find the right solutions for my clients. Once I possessed the right knowledge about the products that could help them it became a simple matter of matching people to answers. I didn't need a fancy sales pitch because I was confident in what I was delivering. I want the same for you.

Gaining that sort of product knowledge in what you have to offer the world isn't only about securing a job, either. It can make you more comfortable in your own skin.

I can clearly remember a sales training seminar I led for all the partners at Arthur Andersen & Co. My job was to teach all the partners how to sell. As I was preparing to deliver this program, I read a quote from a sales psychologist who stated that people spend 94% of their time thinking of themselves. In other words, we are almost always thinking about ourselves – our own wishes, fears, needs, and so on.

That 94% statistic is unfortunate, particularly if you want to work in sales. High-level selling isn't really about delivering glossy presentations or talking other people into doing things they don't want to do. It's not like in the movies where the polished sales-person will wow the client with a masterful "close" that pushes a deal over the finish line. Instead, good sales technique is about finding people whom your products and services can help. It involves a lot of listening. You can't be an effective listener, though, if you are focused on your 94% and not what the other person is truly feeling and perhaps not expressing.

In theory, putting our own mental and emotional junk aside should be as easy as making a decision to shift our attention. But our brains don't really work that way. We are utterly incapable of focusing on someone else's concerns until we can quiet the chatter in our own minds. This is where knowing yourself makes the game a whole lot easier.

The "94%" has been a key coaching concept of mine since I learned of it. This concept is so crucial that I want you to remember its definition as you read the rest of the book. You might even want to mark this page and come back to it when you see "94%."

When you figure out who you are as a person and a professional, and learn to actually be *comfortable* with those realizations, you are able to put them aside. Only then can you lock in on what another person is telling you without obsessing on what it means for you every few seconds.

Personal product knowledge allows you to unlock this hidden ability. Once you have it you are able to communicate more effectively, become more persuasive than other individuals, and connect with people in a way that makes you more memorable and attractive to them. Those are all traits you want in an interview, once you're working within a company, or even further down the road when you move into a leadership position.

One other thing to note about self-discovery is that it can bring purpose to your work. A greater awareness of your own needs and tendencies allows you to find and select roles that fit your long-term passions. This helps you set off in the right direction. It also helps you make smarter choices about pursuing networking contacts, continued education, and opportunities for advancement. Millions of us are drifting from one week or job to the next. If you can identify where you are and where you're headed you will have a massive leg up on everyone else around you.

Gathering Product Knowledge Can Be Hard Work

Now that I've given you all the positive reasons you need to assess yourself the way an employer would, it's time for a quick disclaimer: *this all takes work.*

The process of "getting to know yourself" is often thought of as one that involves meditating on a mountaintop, or perhaps backpacking through another part of the world. I don't have anything against those types of experiences, but they aren't required and might not even be helpful. Instead, what I'm going to recommend is a series of exercises designed to help you reflect and uncover insights.

You may be thinking that you picked up this book because you wanted job search tips, not a series of homework assignments designed to uncover what you think you already know. I'm going to beg you once more to give the activities I'm going to outline a few hours of effort and attention. Not only will they help you find the right direction so you can sell yourself to employers, but they can also prevent bigger mistakes down the road.

One of the most common reasons people meet with me is that they find themselves in their 40s or 50s without any sense of what should come next. Some of my clients are successful; others are still looking for a breakthrough in their careers. What many of them have in common, though, is that they did what was easy, logical, or expected when they joined the working world. They didn't go through this process of figuring out their own strengths and wishes. Eventually, they reached a point where the present and future seemed unrecognizable from where they began. Worse, they felt as if they had backed themselves into professional corners.

People in those situations frequently think they are tied down by knots that can't be untangled. That is never the reality, even if it feels that way. What *is* true, though, is that things could have been much easier for them if they would have simply made better choices from the start.

I'll reiterate that most people aren't truly aware of who they are as individuals or professionals. It's easy for them to miss the forest for the trees because they are too close to everything that's right in front of them.

Remember that as you move into the coming exercises. It would be easy to put this book down, to skip over a section, or to go through the motions without really thinking about the steps. I certainly can't stop you from doing any of those things. In fact, no one except you will know whether you take them seriously or not.

At the same time, realize the exercises I'm providing are meant to help you and not me. To put this another way, you will only be hurting yourself if you skip them. I've been working at these ideas for decades. You can get through them in a couple of hours and gain a fresh perspective you might not have had before, or at least feel more confident about the direction you're about to take. Isn't that worth a little bit of energy?

Along the same lines, I want to encourage you to handwrite your answers whenever possible and appropriate. I'm fully aware that no one ever writes *anything* with a pen and paper these days, but I'm not asking you to do it for the sake of nostalgia.

Neurologists have shown that a different part of the mind is activated when we take the time to handwrite letters and notes. We see our own penmanship as a form of artistry and expression. Writing things out by hand also forces us to slow down and really evaluate our thoughts. Also, on a practical level it gives us a point of reference (a written page) we can return to again and again in the future.

There is real magic in pulling ideas out of your mind and putting them into some concrete form. I hope you will take my advice and write out your answers to the exercises given throughout this book.

I will end this brief chapter with a quick word of caution. Even though I want you to take the models and ideas I've chosen for the next chapter seriously, I don't want you to move forward with the expectation that every question or doubt will be cleared up in your mind. They certainly won't.

The reality of life is that plans and conditions are always changing. What you know today will be proven false tomorrow, and even your opinions or beliefs can evolve over time. This book can help you get started in your career but it can't ensure you get everything right.

The upshot is that you will be making choices in an intentional way. Later you might come back and make different or better decisions. At the very least you can learn to make different mistakes rather than following the all-too-common pattern of repeating the same blunders again and again.

Life is a lot easier, and a whole lot more fun, when you accept the fact that you are going to get things wrong pretty often. If I can help you get them *sort of wrong* instead of *completely wrong* then I'll have done my job and will be proud of my work.

I know you might be tempted to skip ahead and figure out how you're going to meet with employers and convince them to hire you. We will get there, but let's take care of the basics first so we can make sure you're headed in a direction that makes sense as you begin.

6

WRITE YOUR LIFE HISTORY

Who are you? What are you good at? What do you really want out of your career, or your life as a whole?

Your career is going to be a journey that lasts 40 years, or in some cases longer. That's quite a voyage. And yet, when I speak with a young person the first time, they are likely to be absorbed by thoughts of what their first or second job HAS to be.

That's because they are filled with fear. They are worried about setting off in the wrong direction, afraid of accomplishing less than their peers, and terrified of disappointing their parents. I try to get them to take a longer view and push those negative thoughts aside. They are at the beginning of something that will take decades. Not every step will be – or even *can* be – the right one.

The first thing to do, if you want to break free of that fear, is take control of the process. Remember, you are the CEO of *MyCo*. You are also its main salesperson and you have a unique product, which happens to be yourself.

Before we can look into the future, we have to study the 20+ years of history around this company and its product. If I were to ask you to evaluate *MyCo* in terms of its background and future prospects right now, how much data could you give me? Usually, the answer is "none," or maybe a few tidbits that were gleaned from a personality assessment done in college.

Let's ask a follow-up question: where do you store the data you do keep? Every young person I work with keeps it in their head. I have worked with a lot of businesses. I feel confident telling you that you will never find the CEO of a successful organization who didn't have good records that were written, organized, and saved in a specific place. Even if they couldn't spontaneously share all the details around previous successes and failures, they would know where to find them.

That analogy brings us back to the situation you are facing with regard to your career. How can you build a strategic plan for *MyCo* if there is no data to guide you? Without data we can't do any analytics. Without analytics we have no plan. And once again, with no plan there is no control.

This is precisely why so many young people feel out of control in the job market.

Your first exercise, then, is to write a life history. You can come up with your own way to do it. I'll tell you, though, that for me the best way to do this is to buy a spiral-bound notebook and write your initial story only on the right-hand pages. When you go back over this story, maybe in a day, maybe in a year, you can then write new thoughts or perspectives on the left side. In this way you can see what you've written but keep expanding on your story as you go.

There isn't one set way to complete this task, but I recommend beginning with a focus on:

- Any recollections of the first six to seven years of your life – What was your childhood like? What could you say about your most vivid memories?
- Your teenage years through high school – Think about your family. What are they like, and how have they influenced you? Do you like researching, writing reports, or working on group projects? Were there certain classes or activities that grabbed your attention?
- College years – Can you think of specific professors or mentors you connected with more easily than others? What was it about them that made learning easy? What was your social life like? What did you do to "chill"?
- Early job(s) – What kind of work experience have you had to this point? You can include part-time jobs, internships, or even informal roles. It doesn't matter whether you've been paid or not; just consider what you have done and how it has affected you.

As you go, remember that your story isn't just about the facts. Context and emotion matter a great deal. Try to recall and include the types of friends you made, the teachers who did or didn't connect with you, and key decisions you had to make along the way... as well as why and how you made them.

There will be other areas you want to explore as well. It's your life history to tell. Don't worry about what is relevant to your career for now. Just get to the heart of where you've been and how it has led you to this point in your life.

As you write the history, you *do not* necessarily have to draw any conclusions. In fact, as you do the writing it might be better if you don't even try. The point of the exercise is to externalize thoughts and move them from mind to paper. This is your chance to express the many dimensions of who you have been as a person, leading to the person you are now.

Once the story has been written, put it away for a few days. Then, you can return to it and use it in a number of ways. One is to simply read it over several times to draw out observations that might hint at the job or career you want. In a separate area of your notebook, begin to note down the characteristics of your ideal job based on reading your own history. If you are very extroverted, you may want to read your life history aloud to a friend, or to your dog or a plant, especially if there are some very private or painful memories involved. The important point is to *engage* with your own material to find insights and self-learning.

This data then becomes your springboard to better understanding yourself as well as guessing (that's right: *guessing*) at what you want in your next job. Until we do this, we can seem like strangers to ourselves. All this data, then, gets poured into the foundation of your career. You can better answer questions like: *who am I, really? What do I want? And how do I get it?*

Don't worry, you aren't expected to have the answer to that final question yet. I'm going to share a creative process that will lead you to new employment opportunities later in the book.

As I said at the beginning of this section, your career is likely to be a 40-year marathon. My best "students" realize this is not a single event to write their life history and then to land the perfect job in one step. NO! You have to continue to capture key events and learnings at work (and in life) simply to hold on to your sanity and remain in control of *MyCo*. So, please, heed this advice and continue to compile data that will allow you to be running an award-winning company.

Lastly, please ponder the fact that your work life is not separate from the other parts of your life. The pieces all need to be integrated. For example, the "whole you" contains aspects like:

- Your marriage or love life
- Your spiritual life
- Your family now and your original family
- Avocations that might still be present such as piano, journalism, pottery
- Leisure time activities such as sports, exercise, socializing

As we become better at running our "company," we come to better understand how integrated these pieces truly need to be if we want to realize our potential.

This exercise could easily take you a couple of hours. It might even require a few days. I know you're anxious to start contacting employers, but I hope you'll take the time to treat this activity very seriously. Remember you can't sell what you don't know and understand, and most of us know more about our favorite sports team or television show than we do our own selves. Looking back is a great way to pivot toward the road ahead.

7

PUT SCIENCE ON YOUR SIDE

C an a standardized test tell you everything about your personality and future? No. But the right personality assessment model *can* give you some insights into your own talents and tendencies.

Most readers of this book will have some knowledge about their own personality type from a test administered during their time at a college or university. If you haven't, however, I recommend the Keirsey Temperament Sorter tool, which is a short form of the longer Myers-Briggs assessment. I also highly recommend a book called *Please Understand Me* by David Keirsey and Marilyn Bates. I have used it with hundreds of young people over the years. It's packed with great information and has an easy questionnaire in the appendix that helps you identify your Myers-Briggs type. You can also view this information online at typelogic.com.

No matter how you get the information, you will eventually be identified as belonging to one of 16 different personality types. If you take the questionnaires seriously there is a high probability that you will be given a score that either matches your personality type or is very close. You will know this because some of the traits described will resonate with you instantly.

Knowing your personality type is valuable in a couple of ways. First, it helps you add more data to your "Who am I?" inventory. It can sometimes be the case that reading about yourself in an abstract, third-person way can bring you focus and clarity you wouldn't have found otherwise. Also, most resources that test your personality type hint at ideal occupations for each type. Obviously, you can disregard those suggestions if none of them seem right, but they can be helpful for narrowing your "what do I want?" list.

If you really want to give your current and future career prospects a boost, you could become an expert on not only your own pattern but also the other 15. Doing so will give you valuable insights into every person you meet or deal with in the future. You could even better understand your beloved author (me!) by reading up on the ENFP pattern.

Obviously, we could fill several books with details on personality types alone. That's not what we're aiming for here, but I do want to give you a simple way to get started. I've always found it easier to summarize the 16 Myers-Briggs patterns into four temperaments. Let's take a quick look at each one:

The SJ Temperament – Around 40% of all Americans fall into this category. The SJ tends to be the institutional caretaker. These are people who are serious, organized, and dependable. They are drawn to clear rules and hierarchies, often working in service to others.

SJs have an accompanying need for control. It appeals to their rule-bound nature. Their learning style tends to be methodical, logical, and linear. These folks like concrete facts and present-tense situations. For them, today is what matters. So SJs have trouble with change since their greatest strength revolves around a routine way of doing things. They are most likely to need help in doing a "to be" model of what they want when they feel dead-ended at work. SJs need to turn to their Board of Directors to explore a new and different "end state."

The NF Temperament – This is where I live, and I can tell you it's filled with some rather strange people. NFs strive for self-actualization. We want to reach our full potential, so we never stop trying to grow and develop into something new. As a consequence, the NF often lives in the magical world of Tomorrowland.

Authenticity and genuine relationships are important to this personality type. They like total honesty with no pretense. Career planning can be incredibly difficult for this group (I'm living proof) until they come to understand that it is almost impossible to ever settle on a "final destination" career choice – that would be breaking the cardinal rule of always working to become something different and better.

The NT Temperament – This temperament only makes up around 12% of the population. Ironically, I work with them regularly because NTs tend to become the physicians, leaders and scientists who make up the bulk of my coaching work.

The NT likes to deal with the Latin *animus*, which involves the logical, thinking mind. The scientific method is a wonderful expression of the NT trait. They like to generate hypotheses, test them, and arrive at evidence-based conclusions. From a career perspective, the greatest strength of NTs can become their greatest weakness, i.e., they can fiddle and diddle endlessly with diagrams of the "better mousetrap," yet not act. They need to settle on a career model and launch the search.

The SP Temperament – This type is not often seen in corporate America, probably owing to the fact that freedom is their most essential quality or aspiration. These are people who don't want to be tied down.

The defining quality of an SP is a tendency to act on impulse. They crave action and simply want to be free to do whatever they damn well please. Many actors, painters, artists, and performers fall into this category.

Please note that there is no such thing as a "best" temperament. We need all of them, and there are tremendous career possibilities for every variation. What I hope you'll take from this section is that it's important to learn what you can about your own type. Then, you can graduate to studying other styles and grow as a colleague and leader.

Finally, don't forget you should have sections in your notebook related to the questions "Who am I?" and "What do I want?" This would be a good time to update those. In fact, these parts of your notes should keep changing, and hopefully becoming more focused, as you continue through these pages.

8

WHERE DO YOU FIT IN?

S cience can tell you quite a bit about yourself. However, there's nothing quite like checking in with your own intuitions. Usually your gut feelings will confirm what you learned from a Myers-Briggs assessment. However, in my experience it is the internal realizations that drive us forward, not the formal studies or reports that give us the same information.

With that in mind, this chapter includes a pair of exercises I have used with young people again and again. They are simple but tend to be revealing. They don't just uncover more clues about the directions you should take, but may also give you hints about which roles or career paths you might want to avoid.

To help you understand why those insights are so valuable, I will share another brief story from my own life. Although it was decades ago, I can still vividly remember my one job interview on campus at Bowdoin. I was a senior at the time and a counselor had arranged for me to meet with the representative from a well-known tire company.

The trouble began when, in preparation, I took a bus from my suburban home to Boston the week before the interview. I wanted to see how long the commute would take. During my ride I sat next to dozens of other commuters. While a few got on or off the bus at each stop, mostly they all sat silently reading newspapers with a joyless look on their faces. I couldn't imagine grinding my life away like that for decades.

That morning commute test run haunted me. Things only got worse on the actual day of the meeting. You would think that my one and only job prospect would have been sitting at the front of my mind. Maybe it should have been. Instead, I forgot about the interview altogether and was 10 minutes late. Not only that, but I was sweating profusely from a touch football game I had hurried in from.

The young interviewer was gracious enough not to comment on either of these things. Instead, he asked me a simple question: "So, why do you want to be in the rubber business?" With that one simple query I folded like a cheap suit. I answered that I was sorry, but a job with his company wasn't for me. So, after being late and unprepared, I got up and walked out of the room less than two minutes in.

I feel bad that I wasted that man's time, but the event was actually a learning experience for me. In that moment I came to two important realizations.

The first thing I realized when I sat down with the interviewer was that I didn't want to be another cog in a big business wheel. The second is that I would never, *ever* be able to last in a job where I had to tell people I was "in the rubber business."

You don't need that kind of cringe in your life, either. So, let's figure out where you might fit in the working world with a pair of intuitive exercises.

Choose a Lap to Run

I want you to imagine for a moment that I was going to sign you up for a relay race. This wouldn't be a normal race, though. I wouldn't do that to you – there might be "exercises" in this chapter but none of them should cause physical sweating. No, this race would be one that would test your skills for creativity, planning, execution, and concentration.

Specifically, the race would be to design a dream house with an imaginary client. You would be assigned to one of four different laps. The responsibilities would be broken down like this:

Lap One – This person's job would be to meet with the client and gain their trust. The Lap One individual would have to help them feel safe in sharing their vision for the future. They would need to dream together with the client about all the different possibilities for this home, and make sure the client was excited about them before the project could move forward. Those who struggle to connect or be persuasive would have a hard time with this role.

(To bring this back to the story I opened the chapter with, I have come to understand myself as a 100% Lap One person. So much so that any standard routine such as a daily commute to the same place with the same people would never be satisfying. I need to be meeting new people and architecting new projects all of the time!)

Lap Two – The second of our racers would work as an architect. This individual's task would be to take the big dream that was passed on from the first lap competitor and turn it into a realistic blueprint. Part of this job would be scaling back those big plans and ideas that were dreamed up into something more tangible and then getting agreement from the client that the revised plan was the best way forward.

Lap Three – The person picking up the baton for the third lap of the race would need to supervise the actual construction of the dream home itself. They would be responsible for keeping the project on time and within budget while juggling the needs and setbacks given to them by others. This would be a difficult role for those who weren't natural leaders or had trouble making decisions.

Lap Four – This lap would be handled by a specialist who wanted to get hands-on and concentrate on their own work. Generally this person would be someone who was very good at what they do, but liked to avoid conflict and the burdens of management. In this role, the competitor could focus on their own responsibilities without having to incorporate another person's unrealistic ideas or expectations.

So, ask yourself: which lap would I want to handle? In some cases you might be suited for more than one, but most people aren't going to be a great fit for all the roles. In fact, the majority of us are going to have a primary and secondary preference.

The beauty of this exercise is that it's a simple way to think about the types of work you are likely to enjoy, as well as the sorts of jobs or positions you might want to avoid. In Lap One, for example, you tend to find a lot of successful salespeople. Lap Two individuals could be literal architects, as well as planners and organizers. Lap Three attracts managers and executives, while Lap Four is the biggest group – specialists and workers who want to focus on their own skills and areas of expertise.

There are literally millions of types of jobs out there, but most of them correspond to one or two of the simple role types I've outlined here. Give some thought to which ones you have gravitated toward in the past, and how they may or may not be a good fit for you moving forward.

Are You a Box Stepper or a Box Jumper?

Suppose that as part of a job interview I asked you to put together a physical model made out of plastic blocks. Your ability to move on to the next stage in the hiring process would be dependent on the successful completion of the task. You would be working with a time limit, but one that didn't require you to rush.

Are you the kind of person who would read all the instructions and follow all the steps in order? Or, would you be likely to skip ahead once the process and desired results were clear?

There isn't a right or wrong answer to this question. It's simply a way to think about one aspect of your personality.

Some people are *box steppers*. By that I mean they finish all of the activities in a given box, and make sure they understand the relevant ideas, before moving on to the next step. These are the logical thinkers who make up a good two-thirds of the population.

On the other side of the coin you have *box jumpers* like me. They can see ahead to conclusions very quickly but struggle to follow defined steps or processes. To them, the instructions are an annoyance rather than a helpful guide.

Again, most people aren't purely one thing or another. But, by recognizing your own box stepping or box jumping tendencies you can go a long way toward figuring out what sort of career path is going to suit you. Box steppers tend to like structured environments where tasks are clearly defined. Box jumpers can work in chaos but don't want to be held back by rigid rules. In which group do you belong?

The Difference Between Interests and Roles

There are a lot of people who would rather be in the rubber business than work in a private school. And likewise, some of you
might think you could be fascinated by the science behind tires or
bored to death by the details of life insurance policies. That's all
fine. The point isn't to disparage any job or industry, even if I'm
having a bit of fun with them. The bottom line is that each of us
fits somewhere, but those fits aren't always predictable.

You might have topics you are interested in, but I don't want you to
confuse a subject or industry with a role. In the same way that you
can live in a great house or a terrible apartment without switching
cities, you could have the perfect job or the worst fit all in the
same company.

This is a good thing to remember as you go along in this book, and
later as you progress through your career. You might come across
people who recommend a job track in tech, or the pursuit of poli-
tics (as examples). Those could be the right choices for you, or
they might not. What is most likely to determine your happiness
and success, however, is finding your place within the field or
organization you're pursuing. Box jumpers shouldn't try to be
steppers, and someone who is best suited to Lap One of a race
won't be happy if they are competing with others in Lap Four.

I think you get the idea. The point of these exercises was to help
you further refine and validate what you have already learned
about yourself (don't forget to update your "Who am I" and "What
do I want" information). In the next chapter we are going to step
back and look at things from the other side. If these exercises were
focused on the micro of today's tasks and skills, then I want you to
consider a longer timeframe... and even your career destiny.

9

YOUR CAREER DESTINY

One of my favorite questions to ask a coaching client goes something like this: "I know you don't have the answer to your problem, but if you did what would it be?"

At first glance that can seem like nonsense. *Of course* the client doesn't have a solution. If they did, they wouldn't be talking to me. But sometimes, with a little bit of creative probing, you can set up an inquiry like this and get dramatic results. People know more than they think, particularly when they have taken the time to really explore a topic in their own minds.

That's a good reminder for me to extend at the beginning of this chapter because I'm going to ask you to be a little bit assumptive. You might not know the future or believe in any divine higher power. And yet, by thinking creatively for a moment as if you did, you might be able to generate some amazing insights into your own dreams and talents.

So, are you ready for another Timbo-imagined exercise? If so, then let's look a little further into the future.

The Age 75 Looking Back Exercise

This is an exercise I came up with many years ago while searching for a bit of clarity. I realized I would often get stuck, as many do, when my path forward was cloudy. In other words, if I didn't know what I was working toward, it got hard to keep plugging ahead. So, I decided to pretend I could see farther over the horizon. Now I'm going to ask you to do the same.

As with the other creative activities I have given you to work on, the point of this exercise isn't to be 100% realistic. I want you to daydream a little bit. That means (once again) this exercise is going to be easier for those of us with imaginative temperaments. If you're the kind of person who likes concrete information then I hope you will give this a try. Maybe even consider phoning a friend.

Here is how the exercise works: you imagine that you are closing in on your 75th birthday. As the day draws near a loved one announces they want to throw a huge bash in your honor. All the details are up to you. It can be anywhere you want, you can invite anyone you would like, and the food, drinks, and entertainment will be taken care of. All you have to do is write a speech for everyone who will be in attendance and tell them what you think of your life and achievements so far.

Want a sample to work from? I first completed this exercise myself in 1981. I imagined myself on a sweeping wraparound porch with a view of a serene lake. I would be surrounded by my family, friends, and a handful of my closest clients. Here were the key points from the speech I planned on giving...

"Folks, I did it my way! It took some work learning to better balance the different parts of my life and to figure out how to focus on what mattered. But in the end I was able to make a wonderful living doing a job that captured all my creativity, passion, and purpose."

At this point I want you to remember that as I wrote those words I had yet to discover that I wanted to work in coaching. In fact, this exercise helped me find that extra bit of direction in detail.

Next up were people from three different generations talking about how they couldn't have grown without my care, concern, and genuine love. Then it was time for me to continue my speech.

"I'm so proud to have written humorous and poignant books that have helped so many people live better lives. And just look at my kids and their kids! Everyone is so healthy, and they are all carrying on with the great values they got from me. Mostly I'm just proud to have cared for others more than I selfishly cared for myself. One of the most important things to me has been that I've mattered to a large number of people, and have been blessed to have so many good friends. I'm also happy that I've stayed in great physical shape and am still able to play squash every week."

Now, you might be saying this would be a bit weird as a speech. You're right. However, what I've really done is list several different things – doing things my way, making a good living, living my purpose, starting a family, caring for others, having friends, and staying in great shape – that I wanted to be able to look back on with pride.

In a strange way, looking forward like that can help you clear up your priorities. Then, you can use the knowledge of what you actually care about most to draw things back to the present and start making more immediate plans.

A Leap of Faith

This is another of my favorite exercises that draws on a similar point of creativity. It encourages you to stretch even farther than the 75th birthday model did. But before I give you the details, I have to introduce a quick disclaimer.

I received almost all of my pre-university education in Catholic schools. The teachings were fear-based, and laced with many, many strict *do not's*. It's important to note this upfront because I want you to understand that I am not trying to push my religion on anyone. In fact, there's a chance I'm pushing some of you away with what I have shared so far.

However, I do have to say that the practice of prayer, and forging a connection with a higher power, has given me some sense of peace. And, I would even say it has helped me with my career search... but not because I ever planned on becoming a priest.

One of my favorite bible stories involved a master who gives his three workers talents (money) to care for. The first wastes his, and the second buries what he has in the ground to keep it safe. But the third invests his talents wisely, earning the praise and approval of his master. The point of this parable is to use your gifts in a way that serves you and the world at the same time.

That brings us to this exercise. Regardless of whatever religious beliefs you may or may not have, play along for a moment and imagine a higher power has created you for something special. What are those talents? And how can you best use them – both to have a great life and to fulfill your bigger purpose?

When I went through this exercise as a younger man I developed a crystal-clear picture of what I could and should become: a down-to-earth coach and advisor, armed with a sense of humor and a bit of insight, who could help others in this marathon called life. I saw that this path could leave me at peace with myself but also helping others accelerate their own development.

Personally, I believe that every one of us is here for a reason. Even if you won't ever have any desire to attend mass with me I hope you'll think through this exercise and think about what a higher power would have mapped out for your life. You might be amazed at what you come up with.

Finding Passion, Purpose, and Direction

You will spend a long time working in your career. Shouldn't you spend those long hours, additional trainings, and bursts of effort on something that brings you joy and fulfillment? Wouldn't it be better if you fulfilled your purpose, whatever that is, or at least affected the world in a way that made you feel positive?

For some, the two exercises I have outlined in this chapter will feel abstract. Certainly, I recognize that it's impossible to look decades into the future with any clarity. I'm living proof of that. And, you might not feel particularly compelled to introduce prayer or higher powers into your career planning process. That's also fine.

However, by considering the possibility that you could be designed and destined for something amazing – along with the eventuality that you *will* get older whether you want to or not – you can gain more clarity and control over a huge part of your life. The talents you were born with will stay with you whether you use them or not, and years are going to pass one way or another. Would you rather be the kind of person who drifts along from one part of life to another, or someone who takes control of his or her own destiny?

Some of this might not seem all that relevant to you in the moment. After all, you could just be looking for a job that offers far more pay or better advancement opportunities. Even if that's the case I hope you'll spend a few minutes with these exercises. They could pay off in a big way at some point in your future. If nothing else, they can serve as reminders of how important it is to steer your own ship into the future.

Once you have finished them and made some notes, it will be time to move on to the final exercise in this set. It's definitely one of my favorites. Are you ready?

By the way, please note that I will have finally written just *one* book before hitting age 75 instead of the many books I predicted in 1981. Oh, well!

10

THE IDEAL JOB SCENARIO

The next exercise is one that can be extraordinarily valuable. However, I will warn you in advance that getting the most from it requires you to turn off the critical part of your brain for a little while. Rather than worrying about what's possible or realistic, I want you to live in the land of fantasy until we're done. If you can stick with that rule and dream vividly with all your might, it will be worth it at the end.

With that little disclaimer out of the way, here is how the ideal job scenario works...

To begin, I want you to imagine that an eccentric internet billionaire has invited you for coffee. When the meeting begins, she tells you that she has heard about you and really admires your attitude and effort. However, she can see that you have been struggling to gain any traction in your career.

For this reason, the billionaire has decided to make your success her project. She wants to give you the money and connections you need to live your dreams. However, her offer comes with a couple of caveats. She's not going to just give you a stack of money or a cushy job – she wants you to earn it in a way that best suits your talents and wishes.

In order to do that, she asks you to write down an amount of money – paid annually – that would allow you to not worry about finances at all for the next 10 years. All you have to do to earn this cash is prove that you have worked 40 hours per week, 45 weeks in the year (this altruistic billionaire wants you to have plenty of time off). If you can prove you have done this, she'll keep wiring the money into your checking account year after year.

What sort of work will you do? That's the best part: you can do *anything* you want to. You just have to do *something*. Whatever skills, training, or connections you need she'll take care of. She just wants you work in a role that would bring you happiness and fulfillment. The goal would be to choose whatever felt like the most fun to you. You can collect that money without feeling like you are going to work at all.

There is one last catch, though. The altruistic billionaire wants you to choose your dream job by the end of the meeting. That brings us to the thrust of this exercise, which is to list some ideas about what you would do – remembering, again, that *anything* is possible – AS QUICKLY AS YOU CAN.

Start writing. Don't worry about whether the jobs you list are accessible to you or not. They don't even have to be real. Just add anything you can think of to the list.

There is no need to edit yourself. For the sake of context, I wrote down that I might want to be the Pope, take over for the musician James Taylor, or become a professional athlete. It doesn't matter if you know what these jobs pay, what the qualifications are, or how you get them. Just keep writing. More ideas are better than fewer, and the bigger you think and more outlandish you get the more beneficial this exercise will become.

Once you can't think of any more dream jobs, start to put them in order of preference. Figure out what your biggest dream is, then your second, and so on. The exact rankings aren't that important, but figuring out which ones really set you on fire is.

And finally, you can complete this exercise by expanding on each of your choices and asking yourself *why* each particular job popped into your mind. This is where the magic happens. You might not be on the way to becoming a rock star, but it could be that you have a flair for entertainment or a desire for public recognition. Maybe a position as a video game tester would be tedious and low-paying in the real world, but would give you the chance to compete with others or work with products you love.

This exercise will be easier for some than others. As an NF temperament, I'm a dreamer by nature so this kind of freestyling is a blast. If you are more of a concrete-thinking SJ, then it might take a little more effort to open up your imagination. But please try! I can still remember creating this drill many years ago and coming up with 38 possibilities. I realized at the time that only two of the jobs I listed could be viewed as real, but the insights around them led to a *eureka* moment that guided the next 35 years of my career. It gave me the direction and grounding I needed.

Let me explain. I had no idea whatsoever what I would do after my life insurance sales career came to an end. But one of the 38 entries on my list was to work at Dartmouth College. Why Dartmouth? I liked the location. The college and town seemed like they blended together beautifully, and there was a lovely golf course to play. I could imagine myself as a freshman hockey coach at the school.

When I dug a little bit deeper into those wishes I started to arrive at some firmer conclusions. At 32 years old, my career was at an inflection point. I was a classic "tweener," someone who didn't really fit one definition or another. Half of me was an academic, and the other half wanted to be a businessman. I realized I didn't want to live in either of those worlds full time. I needed to find a way to help develop young people without going back to the classroom.

Now that I had better product knowledge about myself I was able to think more critically about what I wanted to accomplish. So, I went to a local college and looked at their literature on staff roles at different universities (remember, this was in the age of fossils before the internet). I did a bit of homework and then came across the entry I was looking for... *career services*. It was a role that could allow me to help students, but with the things that matter to them (finding a job) and not the things that didn't (my passion for Latin literature).

In that moment I knew I had stumbled upon an answer to my long-term direction. I also concluded that a career services job at Dartmouth would be one I would pursue later in my career because it didn't fit my immediate needs related to geography and finances. That's what happens when you apply theoretical ideas to real life– shit happens and plans change. Still, it gave me a way to understand what I wanted, which pointed me in the right direction for the next few decades of my career.

This is such an important concept that I don't want it to get lost in the bigger story. So, allow me to spell out the biggest point in this book so far. *Drumroll, please...*

1. I had worked very hard on the "Who am I?" piece of product knowledge to pinpoint my best traits. That

allowed me to think about myself objectively, and also built up my sense of self-worth (which was a huge step forward for me).

2. Then, I used the ideal job exercise to clarify the way those best qualities fit together with the "what do I want?" piece of the puzzle. This was HUGE for me. At that point I knew my strengths, felt good about myself, and could actually think clearly about what I wanted.

3. This gave me a clear path forward. I knew I could take the next steps without drifting off in a direction that didn't suit me. From there, figuring out "how do I get it?" was simply a matter of designing and following the right process. Everything flowed naturally from the first two steps.

This is such a crucial sequence of events that I will refer to it at a few different points throughout this book. Most young people feel aimless and out of control because they have no information. The ideas and exercises I'm providing are all about helping you better understand yourself and your ideal future. Once those answers are cleared up, the process of getting started on finding the right job is almost secondary.

To tie a bow on my story, it didn't take me long to visit a former high school classmate who was working at Arthur Andersen (a consulting powerhouse) in Boston. It wasn't Dartmouth, but it was a place where I could use both the business and academic parts of my brain together. The classmate introduced me to his managing partner and the rest is history. I spent a decade consulting with that firm and it set me up for all the great successes that came later.

What is cool about this example is that I basically made up a job where one didn't exist. The executive coaching business wasn't "born" until well over a decade later.

Please, take this drill seriously by being as open, silly, and unrealistic as you can. I owe much of my career success to the time I spent daydreaming about ideal jobs and then figuring out why I wanted them. It is not just me; many young people have told me that this exercise helped them find a new sense of direction, too. So dream on!

11

START KEEPING SCORE

A funny thing happens when my coaching clients start to complete the exercises I've laid out in the first half of this book. Gradually, they go from "no data," or not knowing anything about themselves, to a point where patterns begin to emerge. They begin to see themselves in a new light. Their own strengths and weaknesses become more apparent because they start looking for information instead of instant gut-feel answers.

This progress often helps them determine where their best talents lie. However, it also gives them greater insight into what kind of job opening they want to look for. Can you feel the same thing happening in your own mind? Is it easier to imagine an environment where you would not only punch a clock and receive a paycheck, but also feel successful and fulfilled?

If so, you are on the right track and this exercise is going to be the perfect next step. If not, I don't want you to worry. Go through this activity anyway and just make educated guesses. When it comes to the topic of *MyCo*, your estimates are better than anyone else's.

And besides, you can't afford to sit back and wait for an epiphany to come to you (I'm going to explain why in the next chapter).

The job opportunity scorecard is one of my favorite exercises because it keeps you in the driver's seat of your career plan. It's all about taking the factors that you have identified as being important to you and using them to find the best possible fit.

Getting started is easy. You simply take the major components of a potential future job offer and rank them from most to least important. The specific criteria will be unique to you, of course, but here are some factors my coaching clients usually consider:

Daily Tasks and Responsibilities – What would you actually be doing in the job? Could you see yourself enjoying the work and growing into your role?

Skill and Personality Fit – Is the job itself a good fit for your skill set and temperament? Does it match up with your learning and working styles?

Educational Fit – Do you have the right background to perform this job? The answer might not be as cut and dried as you think. Often, college (or other) education is much less relevant than interest or work ethic, particularly for entry-level positions.

Mental and Physical Challenges – Is this an office job? Is it a hands-on position that requires lots of movement and activity? Will you be inside or outside? What about travel?

Chain of Command – Whom would you be reporting to, and how do you feel about the person? Remember that having the right boss is a huge factor in job satisfaction.

Company Culture – Do you agree with the mission of the company? Is the organizational culture a good match for your style and values?

Location and Surroundings – Where would you be located? Could you see yourself working productively in the office or facility? Is the commute acceptable, and is the position in a part of the country or world where you would like to live?

Advancement Opportunities – What is the pathway forward for you to advance beyond your starting role? It's okay to get creative when thinking about this question. Even if there aren't direct advancement opportunities, the right job can open doors within a company or industry that aren't immediately obvious.

Salary and Other Benefits – While salary and benefits considerations aren't usually critical for entry-level jobs, it's a lot easier to get by with a healthy paycheck, paid vacations, and so on. Plus, lots of employers are adding extra perks (like free lunches) these days. These aren't usually make-or-break items on your scorecard, but they can be useful to think about in certain situations.

Note that these factors aren't being given equal weight. In fact, you might not consider some of them at all, either because they aren't important to you or because the job opportunities you will be seeking will all be so alike. For example, someone who wants to work in a university library may have a similar work environment wherever they go, and salaries may not differ greatly from one region or institution to the next. In that instance other factors would be considered as tiebreakers.

Along the same lines, there might be some decision criteria that are much more important to you than anything I've listed here. That's perfectly fine. Just identify the four or five things you think matter most to you and rank them in order of their impact.

Do you want to make a ton of money, or is it more important to you to live in a vibrant city? This is a good time to decide. Would you be miserable working in an office, or do you need to be part of a close-knit team of coworkers you get along with? Think about what matters to you and then write it down.

This exercise is valuable because it forces you to think critically about what you want before you go looking for openings. It also gives you a framework for evaluating and comparing different job offers. If you follow the advice I'm going to share and turn yourself into the top salesperson for *MyCo*, then you are going to attract some interest from employers.

By the way, this work will have a dual purpose when you are out interviewing. I want you to turn this document into a genuine scorecard with a weighted system so you can evaluate which jobs will be the best fit. It is amazingly helpful. I have provided an example of a scorecard like this in the appendix.

12

BEFORE WE MOVE ON

Every coaching and consulting client is different. However, the vast majority share a common trait: they are in a huge hurry to get to the answers. This is a particularly strong tendency among younger people.

I get that. When you're struggling with a huge problem (like career confusion) that feels like it could define the rest of your life, then you want it solved *pronto*. Unfortunately, getting to the solutions you need isn't usually as simple as running through a few checklists. The human mind isn't that basic. Change almost always comes from the inside out. That's why the questions and exercises I've given you are so essential to this process.

The huge mistake people make at all stages of their career is to focus on *how* and *when* at the exact moment they should be asking themselves *what* and *why*.

To that end, let me pull you back to my three-step formula: get to know yourself, decide what you want, and then execute a plan to sell yourself to employers. Everything I've shared to this point in the book has been focused on helping you create actionable data around who you are and what you really want to do. That's important... probably more important than you realize. And yet, most of the people you will ever meet don't take the time to follow this path. Instead, they charge ahead and try to land a job with little or no analysis. Is it any wonder they end up in roles that don't suit them?

If you have been following along like a good coaching student or client then you should understand some things about yourself that you didn't know when this journey began. You have more data than most of your peers, and hopefully a sense of one or two directions you might want to pursue. In that case you're ready to take the ice.

However, if you have flown through the earlier chapters in a rush to reach this point, then I want you to go back and start again. Put yourself in the penalty box. Fill in any gaps you might have missed. I know you're dying to get to the super-secret handshakes and passwords that will help you land the job of your dreams. But you aren't ready for that yet. Learning about sales won't help you if *MyCo* has no plans, no products, and no leadership.

In fact, even if you *have* done all that I've asked you might want to take a quick refresher on what you came up with for the "Who am I" and "What do I want" pieces. Not only do these need to be complete, but there shouldn't be any inconsistencies between them. They should flow cleanly from one to the other.

Because the next section is devoted to the "how do I get it" stage of the process, I'm going to make the assumption that you've done the work required. Skipping important steps will only hurt you and/or your progress.

Got that? Great. In the next phase of the book we will learn all about how you can approach the job search differently than your peers. I'm going to teach you why the best jobs are never advertised online, why the best salespeople never actually *sell* anything, and the way you can use these two pieces of knowledge to push your career forward. But first, you need to understand why the old way of finding a job can be so frustrating.

We'll get to that in a couple of pages. But first, I want you to hear from someone who *isn't* closer to retirement than graduation.

Haley's Story

Showing is always better than telling, especially when you want someone to follow your advice. That is something I have been keenly aware of as I have been writing and editing these chapters. It's easier to learn from someone who has walked in your shoes recently, and harder to relate to another person's experiences when they come from another era. But on the other hand, the new and recent graduates who are in your shoes don't have the experience or perspective to teach you how to sell themselves.

Or, if we wanted to be less abstract about it, one of the biggest questions in this book boils down to: how can you be sure you should listen to an old guy who hasn't had to find a job for a while?

I thought the best way to bridge the gap would be to introduce you to someone who has been coached by me personally, gone through the steps and activities I describe, and come out the other side. Want to know what it's like to work the *MyCo* plan before you jump in? This is your chance.

To get that different perspective I turned to Haley, a 25-year-old who recently made some career changes.

Haley was a blast to work with. Her Myers-Briggs pattern was clearly the NF temperament. Her underlying need was to self-actualize, or simply to be the very best she could be. She was also a wild woman "box jumper" whose mind would naturally race ahead to solutions whenever possible. I helped her use that talent to think about the future standards by which she would judge success or failure in her life and career.

The interesting thing about Haley was that her greatest strength, emotion, could also become her greatest weakness if it wasn't properly directed. She had a deep fear that she would never find the right path. The emotional force of that fear would push back against her own ambition. The results were uncertainty and self-doubt.

What Haley ultimately came to understand in our time together was that she needed to focus on her one big desire, which was to help others. With that piece in place her other struggles started to melt away. Her driven, dynamic, extroverted, and funny personality started to shine.

Haley is a truly special person. It's amazing watching her grow into her potential, and I'm excited to see what she will accomplish in the future. I'll be spreading some pieces of her story throughout the remainder of this book. A few names and details have been changed or obscured to protect the guilty, but otherwise this is Haley's story in her own words...

I was incredibly lucky to find an internship with a well-known manufacturing company during my senior year of college. By the time I graduated I had made some relationships with the people I was interning for. I seemed to fit in well with what they were doing so they offered me a job.

It was a great way to get into the working world. I was involved in the hiring and training process for an industry leader. Some days that meant helping with interviews. Other times it was developing training programs or working to identify future leaders who could be promoted down the road. Every week was fast-paced, but I love being in the middle of all the action. I was learning a lot and had a great relationship with my boss. She really got me. She seemed to have a knack for getting my best work from me when she needed it, and then laying off before it became overwhelming. I really enjoyed coming to work and was learning so much.

If you would have asked me a couple of years ago, I would have told you I was never going to change jobs. I would have gladly stayed with the same company for many years to come. But things changed pretty quickly. New leadership came to our division and the boss I loved working for was transferred. Schedules and priorities were shifted. The culture of the company moved in another direction and there were more demands put on all of us. Suddenly the long hours I had put in before started to wear on me. There wasn't a single moment when I realized it was time to move on. It was more like I stopped being excited to come to work and began daydreaming about other options over a period of several months.

I wasn't really sure what to do. It was getting hard to show up every day for a job that I didn't find rewarding. But at the same time I didn't want to quit a good job if I didn't have a good reason, and I certainly didn't want to leave without having something else lined up. Was I in a bad situation or just being picky? It was tough to look at things from an objective point of view. I found myself going around in mental circles over and over.

This is where Tim came into the picture. He was already a family friend. One of my relatives mentioned that he knew quite a bit about career counseling and recommended that I have a chat with him. I wasn't sure he would be able to help, but I was tired of going through the same loops in my mind. So I reached out and asked if he would meet with me. He agreed and we set a time.

Even though I didn't know what to expect, our meeting was full of surprises. When you're coming out of school lots of people want to give you advice about your life and career. Most of it is pretty generic. Your parents and friends say things like "work hard" or "get in with a good company." But that doesn't really help you when you're confused, or when you already have a job with an established employer and you don't like what you're doing.

After Tim invited me into his office I worried he might give me one of those speeches. But instead, he introduced himself, gave me a two- or three-minute summary of his background, and then pulled out a yellow legal pad. Then he asked me a lot of different questions and took notes as we went along.

I had come prepared to discuss my resume, or to talk about what I should be doing in interviews. But we didn't spend much time on things like that. He asked me where I had come from and what my passions were like. I spent a while telling him stories about my time on the college basketball team and what my friends were like.

From there, he asked me to think about what my dream job might be. Not a nice job, but what I would do if absolutely nothing were off the table. It was really hard to answer. I probably hadn't thought of anything like that since I was in fifth grade. It reminded me of seeing a guidance counselor who asked me what I wanted to be when I grew up. Most of the jobs I came up with were ridiculous. I said I wanted to be a play-by-play sports announcer, or maybe the president. I felt embarrassed to even blurt those words out loud. It seemed like we were wasting time talking about jobs I was never going to have. Tim told me not to worry about that, and that it was perfectly fine to go "over the top" with my thinking.

For the next step, he asked me to think about Haley, Inc. What would my one-person company sell if it were real? What would be something my current customer (my employer) would like? What would they wish I sold that I didn't? What was the future of the business?

Those answers made me think about my current situation in a much different light. I realized I had already picked up some marketable skills. I also began considering a longer-term future that went beyond the next job. I had figured my decision came down to staying or leaving. But suddenly I could see that I needed to be thinking about more than that. I wanted to make a choice that would set me up for success many years down the road.

As we went through a few more exercises, several breakthroughs started to take place. By stepping outside of myself and seeing my situation as a disappointing Haley, Inc. quarterly report, I could tell I was moving in the wrong direction. And, with Tim's help, I used the crazy hypothetical dream jobs I had listed to discover some traits I hadn't ever put into words before.

Various patterns of success and frustration suddenly made a ton of sense. I realized that I needed to be recognized for the hours I was putting in. My old boss had done a great job of praising me for my work ethic, but my new supervisor either failed to notice or wasn't the type of person to offer compliments. I could see how I was moving away from the enjoyable parts of my current job and being nudged toward the aspects I wanted to avoid. I also started to understand my need for attention, and even public achievement, in a way that didn't feel embarrassing. Tim explained those were necessary qualities in certain leadership roles, and that they could be motivating.

As silly as it sounds, I was learning about some of my strengths for the very first time. I also gained a great deal of clarity about what it would take to move forward.

13

A BETTER WAY TO FIND A JOB

B efore we dive too deeply into my process for finding the perfect job, let's take a look at the roadmap you've probably used up to this point... along with the reasons it is almost certainly bound to end up in failure.

Most young people, when they enter the working world, are naturally focused on the known job market. These jobs are made available when a company decides they have a position to fill. A *known* job is one that people know about through online listings and other announcements (amazing, right?). With this sort of opening, an employer follows a standard set of steps to find the person they need:

- First, they write a job description that includes information about the company, what position they are hiring for, and the ideal background for an applicant.
- Next, they post this job description in a number of places (for instance, university bulletin boards) where local

candidates might see it. The company does this because they are hoping to hire someone on the cheap.

- The process continues when they post the same job description on some internet employment sites like Monster and Indeed.
- Depending on how successful those efforts were or weren't, the company might continue by placing further ads or speaking to current employees or vendors in the hopes of gaining referrals.
- If none of these methods is successful, they will turn to recruitment agencies and pay a fee to the group that brings in the winning candidate.

On the applicant's side is a mirroring of the same process. The person looking for a job follows a similar series of steps:

- They begin by firing resumes at every company in the area, hoping to hit on one that has a need for their skills at just the right time.
- They talk to all their friends and contacts, asking if anyone knows about a job opening.
- They spend a huge amount of time on sites like LinkedIn and Indeed, looking at employment postings and filling out resume submission forms.
- And finally, they sign up with job search agencies hoping a salesperson with more connections can find the right match or opportunity.

Although the employer and the potential employee are working from opposite ends, they have a lot in common. Both are following a plan of action that is incredibly disorganized and competitive all at the same time. Both parties feel an acute need to make something happen but have little control over the outcome. The whole thing is designed to hope things will sort out in a way that the best candidate – someone who can step in and do the job perfectly from day one – will come through in the end. What happens far more often is that employers settle for people they don't really want and young people accept positions they aren't really suited for. Eventually one party decides to move on to try again and this whole process begins anew.

Despite these failures, the average job seeker spends three-quarters of their time, or more, looking for known jobs. It's a frustrating process that makes it very difficult to differentiate yourself from the millions of other job seekers out there. It leaves many feeling numb to the point that they either want to give up or just settle for the first offer they can attract.

If you have been in this position, or are dreading it in the future, I want you to know I understand. Firing out endless resumes can feel like banging your head against the wall. Even worse, the known job market yields, at best, 20% to 30% of all jobs. That means *most* people end up finding employment some other way. Still, I would encourage you to play in this arena.

Why would I advise you to do something that doesn't have a high probability of success? It's all about time and resources. The only sales and marketing tool you need to compete in the known job market is your resume. So why not put together a few versions and then fire it everywhere? Because you've already done the hard work to understand who you are and what you want, you may be able to generate a solid job opportunity in this way. And then you'll be able to use the consultative selling framework I'm going to share to shine in the interview process.

As you've probably guessed, I don't want you to work *only* in the known job market. I want you to cover your bases there, but to concentrate your mental energy on the opportunities others don't even see. After all, it's a lot easier to get the job you want when no one else even knows it exists.

Jumping Into the Hidden Job Market

It might sound like an impossible task to get a job that doesn't technically exist. I promise you it can be done. The trick is in positioning yourself the right way. I learned the basics of this approach while working for Northwestern Mutual.

Let me explain. Life insurance is one of the hardest things to sell. That's because even though most adults should *have* it, most of them don't actually *want* it. In fact, the people who are actively looking for life insurance are usually the ones who can't get it. That's because the average healthy person isn't especially keen to consider their own mortality, much less set aside money every month so someone else can benefit if they kick the bucket unexpectedly. Conversely, the people who *are* worried about dying – perhaps because they have recently had a heart attack or stroke – will find it difficult to find an insurer willing to take the risk.

The result is a situation where millions of people need life insurance, but don't want to pay for it or even think about it. The natural solution to this conundrum is that a good insurance agent will make connections with men and women who look like their best clients and educate them gradually. They will explain how the right policy can be used to hedge against the unknown and provide peace of mind without breaking the bank. In this way the insurance agent provides real value to someone who has a need they might not have even known existed and certainly didn't want to spend time or energy finding answers to.

We call this process consultative selling, and I will explain it in more depth later. The point I need you to absorb right now is that being effective in sales is often about locating the right person or target rather than responding to market demand. For *MyCo* to grow it won't be enough to simply wait for buyers to come to you.

This concept is the key to the hidden job market. It's based on the practice of building relationships even when there is no need for the employer to hire someone new.

In some ways, this might sound counterintuitive. Why meet with someone who isn't going to hire you? Let's look at the advantages:

- You state up front that it is only a meeting, and that everyone involved "knows" that there is no job. That means there isn't anything for you to feel stressed about. The person you're meeting with doesn't have to feel any pressure to offer you something, either.
- Because there is no job opening, there isn't any need for a resume, either.
- There certainly aren't any competitors for this job, since no job exists.
- The meeting can be short (just 30 minutes), and it's all about establishing a professional relationship. It's just a conversation.

All the problems I described with the traditional employment search process are eliminated once you dive into the hidden job market. That's because it relies on the most important aspect of any sales campaign: *relationships*. The whole process is driven by warm introductions. You aren't competing with dozens or thousands of other applicants anymore, and neither are you a faceless resume that can easily be ignored by an HR manager or algorithm.

When I first explain my job search process, some students and new graduates feel like they are going to be uncomfortable reaching out to new and existing contacts and asking for help. I like to assure them that I'm going to give them the tools that will allow them to take these actions in a way that feels natural to them. Then, I tell them that following up warm introductions is vastly easier than cold calling executives or sending hundreds of resumes into the black hole of the internet.

No matter how you look at it my plan is a lot less stressful than what you have probably been taught to do. It's much more effective, as well. Even better, I'm going to give you a step-by-step plan to follow. But for now I have to offer a quick reminder: this process won't work if you haven't followed steps one and two in my system.

If you don't have a good idea of who you are as a professional, or what it is you actually want, then these meetings will not help you. That's because you won't know whom to meet with and will be unable to discuss your goals and aspirations clearly. At that point you're wasting everyone's time.

The hidden job market can unlock doors and opportunities you might not even be aware of yet. You just don't want to jump into it before you're ready. Assuming that you are, let's move on and see how you can start building a network of potential employers without crawling through hundreds of online job openings every day.

14

MAKE A LIST AND CHECK IT TWICE

I hate it when you read a book and the author portrays themselves as the kind of person who has never made a mistake. So, I've tried to be open about the setbacks and failures I've encountered on my career journey. However, there was *one thing* I got right early on, even if it was by accident. I started my first real job search with a very specific list of potential employers.

You might remember that when I graduated from Bowdoin, I was looking for a place where I could teach Latin at a school that was next to the sea. This campus also had to have a hockey team. A little bit of research at my local library yielded five possibilities. I got hired at the first one I visited even though there were no jobs listed in New England.

To be sure, there was a bit of luck involved. I started by meeting with the hockey coach on the prep school's campus. He knew the coach I had played for at Bowdoin and was open to having an assistant. This newly met coach introduced me to the head of the classics department. That teacher was excited to have someone who could step in and teach Latin so he could move on to a subject that was nearer to his own passions. Together, they had personal motivations to recommend me to the headmaster (I had found a key to their 94%!). The headmaster and I got along instantly, to the point that he asked me to join the school during my visit. I accepted the job offer on the spot!

That's a lot of good fortune for a single cold visit to a potential employer. In retrospect, I probably should have broadened my criteria (but only a little) to include more schools. However, I've been working with job seekers long enough to know that if you stick to the law of large numbers I'll tell you about in the next chapter – finding around 20 solid prospects tied to your model – then something good will happen. In other words, you'll get your good luck, too, if you put yourself in front of enough people. Counting on a good outcome 5% of the time isn't wishful thinking; that's just how probability works.

This chapter is all about taking the first steps in that direction. I'm going to show you how you can build a list of contacts who can help you in your job search. Find enough of them and an unbelievable opportunity will come together for you, just as it did for me.

Let's begin by figuring out what sort of contacts you need on your list.

It's All in Who You Know

Old hands like me are always saying that businesses run on relationships. That's entirely true. However, it doesn't mean you need to be born into a certain family to get ahead, or that you had to go to a prestigious school. Those things can help, but what *really* separates you from everyone else is your personal brand and reputation. In other words, what people think of you, whether they like you, and how much or how little they trust you.

Have you ever seen a movie about the mob? To break into the organized crime ring, an up-and-coming gangster always needs someone else from the established crew who will vouch for them. That's the only way they can be trusted. It's the same in the world of recruiting and employment. You can find a job without referrals, but it's a whole lot harder than having Uncle Vito, or just a trusted executive, tell everyone that you're a good egg.

As we walk through this chapter on finding prospects, we need a term that describes your target. I've always referred to the *Ideal Prospect*. We'll be talking about them a lot, so let's just call them IPs. Each IP can be either a named person, an organization, or both, that fits what you are looking for. Having a description of this IP is the key to unlock the door of the hidden job market.

There are three ways to generate Ideal Prospects. We'll look at each one in turn...but I'll tell you straight away that the third method is simply magic.

Method #1: Market Research

If you are a young person reading this book, then you have no idea how lucky you are. That's because you can get the information you need about potential employers and contacts from anywhere there is a Wi-Fi signal. In *Ye Olde Days* – a.k.a. the era when my job search began and I first started coaching others – learning more about companies meant a trip to the library. Maybe the book you were looking for was on the shelf where it was supposed to be and maybe it wasn't. Perhaps the information was up to date, or possibly not. You just spun the big roulette wheel and hoped for the best.

Things aren't like that now. You could imagine virtually any type of employer and find information about every one of them online. However, that can present a different kind of challenge: information overload. You could potentially research *lots and lots* of employers who might fulfill different criteria on your list. It's important to remember, though, that you don't need huge numbers to succeed. Also, market research is likely to be your least effective form of outreach.

Knowing that, I would advise you to set a reasonable goal. For instance, you might decide you're going to look up 50 potential contacts online. That can give you a great start without being overwhelming.

Note that you don't have to do this work all at once. Whether you prefer a notebook or a spreadsheet, you might break your research down into a few contacts per day, or a handful each week. Depending on how significant your network of contacts is, market research might be the biggest source of prospects for you or the smallest. As I've mentioned, each person or company might represent a low probability of success, but you only need to find one whom you click with. And the law of large numbers tells us that even if you only reach out to a few at a time, you will eventually generate more career opportunities than you actually need.

The list you generate is a list of prospects. Not a single one of them is an Ideal Prospect. This distinction will become clearer in a minute.

Method #2: The Power of Observation

As an insurance salesman I learned to keep my ears and eyes open for any opportunity to generate new business. When you are actively searching for new sales they can seem to come out of nowhere. People tend to think of this as luck, but it's actually basic psychology.

Imagine for a moment that you were a prehistoric human rustling around the bush looking for something to eat. There might be *thousands* of things coming into your field of vision every few minutes. You'd see leaves, grass, birds, clouds, insects, rocks, and all kinds of other items around you. But the hungrier you got, the more things like apples and berries would light up the pleasure centers in your brain. In that environment a human will get better at finding what they are looking for out of simple attention and necessity.

The same thing happens when you are locked in on your job search. You can use your eyes and ears to spot the signs that the kind of job you're looking for might exist. For example, you might walk into a building and notice the list of companies on the directory. Are there any that seem like they could be interesting candidates? At a party you could be paying attention to things other people are saying about their careers and connections.

Not all of your observation has to be personal. Suppose you were looking at a news article about local leaders. Do you see someone you might want to know or model your career after? Could you write that person a letter saying something along the lines of: "I saw the profile about you in the Boston Business Journal (or wherever). I'm running a rather unique job search campaign and have a mental image of the sort of person I would want to work for. I realized it might be you. Would you be open to meeting me for coffee?"

These are just ideas, but the bigger point is that you should always be looking for new ideas and opportunities. Years ago, I worked with a CPA whose dream was to work for a construction company. He had no idea how he could get in with that kind of business, but the idea wouldn't leave him. One day he found himself walking around Boston and came across a crane with the name of a company. So, he stopped someone with a hard hat on and explained what he was trying to do. The construction worker gave my friend a referral. He said, "You should talk to our president. He's a great guy and a former CPA himself." Two interviews later and my client had the position he was looking for.

Good luck is everywhere if you're on the hunt for it. You never know where your next opportunity might come from, but it's bound to appear if you are constantly focused on growing your list of prospects throughout your search. Observation done keenly and actively does result in real live Ideal Prospects.

Method #3: The Magic of Referred Leads

The easiest way to introduce yourself to employers is to have someone else do it for you. That's where referred leads come into play.

When I first began working for Northwestern Mutual all those years ago I had a bit of a conundrum. I truly believed in the product I was selling, and thought it had tremendous benefits for my clients. I also understood that selling insurance was a numbers game on an intellectual level. And finally, I had three young kids at home. All of this is to say that I was highly motivated to find some clients.

The problem? I knew myself well enough to know that I was what you might call a "chicken salesman." I was far too petrified to make cold calls. I had to sell to survive, but I wasn't going to generate leads the way my fearless (or shameless) colleagues did.

I made things work by getting back to what I knew. I was still familiar with the education field and was geographically close to the school where I had earned my master's degree while working as a teaching assistant. So, I made a model of my ideal prospect: a prep school teacher or college-level professor. That was the world I knew. I started reaching out to those folks, in language they understood. The only thing I was selling was a meeting. A chance to meet, greet, and sing my song.

Not only did this approach work, it worked so well that I sold life insurance to more than 150 teachers in my first two years. Then, these folks started referring me to physicians. It turned out teachers and doctors have a lot in common. Both are dedicated to the people they serve, and each group pretends to know everything about everything until you scratch an inch or so beneath the surface. Anyhow, through those referrals I gained more than 100 new clients who worked in medicine. That gave me a new area of specialization.

You can do the same with your sales approach. To get started, you first need to understand and list out all of the people you know and trust who might have access to contacts in your target field or industry. You are searching for people who would help you in any way if they could (see the accompanying chart for ideas). We call these trusted contacts Centers of Influence (CIs).

Once you have identified the right center of influence contacts, you can meet, tell them your story, and ask if anyone comes to mind whom you could meet. These become your referrals. My goal was always to get at least three names from each one. That's because I understood the numbers and knew that if I could keep getting three introductions from each person who knew and trusted me, I would never have to make cold calls (or watch my family starve).

Filling in Your Contact List

Using the three methods I've suggested you should be able to generate at least 20 highly qualified Ideal Prospects to begin with. Whether you put the pieces together on a spreadsheet or a hand-written list is not important. What matters is that you are going to identify at least 20 different individuals or companies who could conceivably hire you for the type of job you want to get.

Although your IPs can be individuals or organizations, it helps if you can narrow your search down to live humans at some point. That might mean finding out who has a certain job within a company you are targeting. This is (once again) easier in the digital age, and it will make your research a lot easier.

You should collect as much background information as possible on each contact. This information will help you establish rapport in the first few minutes of a conversation. There's nothing better to break the ice than something that you have in common, a friend, a favorite sports team or even a town that someone grew up in. Scour company directories, LinkedIn profiles, online articles, and other resources to learn more about each person. Where did they go to school? How long have they worked at your target company? What can you tell about their own values and preferences?

I'm going to go out on a limb and guess that you probably also don't love the idea of calling strangers and asking them for jobs and referrals. None of us loves rejection. I've met a few salespeople who *claimed* that being turned down energized them – telling themselves "every no gets me closer to a yes!" – but they never lasted for very long. So let's assume that's not the best way to do things. The beauty of generating referrals from your Centers of Influence is that it's a great way to create introductions and set meetings without doing things the hard way.

In my sales career, I became adept enough at creating referred leads that it was my primary method for finding new clients. In fact, I sometimes worked backward to generate those introductions – for example, if I had generated 100 names from market research, I would reach out to my contacts to look for connections within my personal and professional circles. Most of the time I could find 10 or 20 who were already known to my friends and clients. Do the same and you'll be amazed at the results!

15

WHO DO YOU KNOW?

W ould you rather be brilliant at finding leads (a.k.a. prospecting) or interviewing with employers?

Let me put that differently: would you rather be a brilliant prospector and a half-assed interviewer, or a half-assed prospector and a brilliant interviewer? I am working very hard in this book to make you brilliant at both. Yet, if I really *had* to choose between those two, the answer would be easy. It would take me half a second to choose to be a brilliant prospector.

Want to know why? It's easy. If a person can generate 20 referrals to their Ideal Prospects, they will find their job. The best interviewer in the known world, with no prospects, is quite literally out of a job. So, you really have to feel the urgency of becoming an excellent prospector. It is the life blood of career success.

It is so bloody simple, but that realization is the hallmark of the brilliant salesperson. Get this one concept down and you will never be lacking for exciting career opportunities. In essence, it is common sense turned into a disciplined science and art. *Focus on generating opportunities*. If you do that enough, the results will come.

I have given you three methods for finding Ideal Prospects, and I truly hope you'll use them all. Each has value and choosing the right one isn't nearly as important as being steady and persistent (remember, you want to be the best at finding leads). However, Referred Leads are where the action is. They aren't just the easiest to work with, but also the most likely to pay off. A Referred Lead is a ball made of gold. You want to have as many of them coming your way as possible.

What Is a Referred Lead?

A Referred Lead is someone who comes to you from a CI, someone who is already known to you. Your CIs have access to people and industries you don't by virtue of their position, location, education, or social background. In other words, they are in contact with your Ideal Prospects.

Just to recap, a Center of Influence (CI) is someone you know who can introduce you to an Ideal Prospect (IP). Still with me?

Knowing that, it's time to find some CIs. It can take hours to scan and examine the people you know and trust who could act as Centers of Influence for you. Let's assume that you are in your early 20s, so some key CIs might be neighbors, friends of parents and family members, high school friends, college professors, classmates, or older graduates of your alma mater. They could also be accountants, attorneys, members of childhood clubs you were a part of, former coaches, or *literally anyone else* you know who has connections with the kinds of people you want to work for.

And don't forget that if your parents or relatives are able to help you, they probably have pretty big networks as well. These are people who know you and like you. They are gold to you. Also please remember that this list of CIs should be ever-growing.

When you start to meet with your CIs, you will be shopping your model of your Ideal Prospect and looking for two things:

1. *Referred Leads*, in the form of actual people they know who fit the profile of what you are looking for.
2. *Other Potential Employers*, who might represent random people they know who could be excellent new CIs after you meet them. You're trying to grow an ever-expanding list of people, so keep looking for introductions!

Please remember that some of the CIs you meet now will remain with you forever if you treat networking like a two-way street. That just means they are helping you while you are *also* looking out for ways to help them. Maybe they have a son or daughter who is looking to work in an area you know something about. You are not too young to have made contacts that others could benefit from. Keep your eyes open and make connections where you can. Create Referred Leads for others when possible.

How to Make Referred Lead Prospecting Work

Please take a moment to pause here and appreciate the magnificence of Referred Lead prospecting. As I've said, it is common sense applied to looking for a job but there are some "tricks" to getting good at it. You should know a few tricks of the trade.

Let's assume you have spent several hours building your CI list. Let's also assume it's comprehensive. I learned the hard way that it is not nearly enough to visit with these close friends and tell them you are looking for work. Neither is it enough to ask if they know of anyone for you to call on. If you did that you would get a resounding "yes" that your friends and family would love to help...

followed by total silence. People want to help, but tend to freeze when they are put on the spot and asked to produce some names of people you can contact. They tense up, find they can't think of a company or a job, and don't know what to suggest. So, the opportunity flames out. Silence!

Let me give you an approach that removes that silence and delivers actual referrals:

Start by relaxing. Simply ask your CI something like: "I assume you would help me on my job search if you could?" They will likely answer: "Of course!" Neither of you is stressed or put on the spot.

Next, paint a picture. Since you know your CI well, take them through the first two steps of identifying your job target; namely, how you went through an examination of who you really are, followed by an outline of your Ideal Prospect. Ask them if they can think of anyone who might align with that profile. Also tell them to not worry about whether there is a job or not. Tell them you are looking to meet with 20 people who fit your profile. Nothing more.

Your CI learns a lot from this description, and will respect the focused way you are approaching your job search. But, sadly, they still won't usually come up with many, if any, Referred Leads if you stop here.

What your CI *really* needs is for you to help by feeding them specific categories of potential names. Tell them where these contacts might come from – something that will be easy for you since you know a lot about your CIs, including clubs they belong to, colleges they went to, friends they have in town, places where they work, who their clients are, who their suppliers are, and so on.

Once you feed your CI these categories, the light bulbs go off! They start to get on a roll. You might get three names from one CI. Awesome! You only need 17 more. Also ask for other folks they might know who might know *even more* actual Ideal Prospects tied to your model.

You are now on a roll, but there is one more critical piece to learn. You don't want your CI to make the introduction to an IP for you. You want to be the salesperson, not your CI. After all, your CI might have every intention of reaching out on your behalf right up until the moment life intrudes on them and forces them to put it off. And off. And off. Then comes the awkward email from you that says, "Oh, I just wanted to ask where you stand with that introduction you were going to make..." UGH.

It is possible that your CI is an excellent networker and wants to approach his referral by himself first. I would not argue with this. If at all possible, however, try to do it yourself.

Simply ask for the specific contact information for the three (or however many) Referred Leads your contact can provide. Then you can show your CI a low-key sample letter or email beginning with a sentence that goes something like: "I was speaking with [CI name] and she thought you would be a great person for me to speak with..."

In a couple of chapters I'm going to show you how to use those letters to maximum effect. But first, you need to know why the approach you're following makes your job search success virtually inevitable.

16

IT'S A NUMBERS GAME

With my apologies to sex workers and cocaine dealers, let me be the first to tell you that very few products actually "sell themselves." Even companies with the most sought-after electronics and luxury cars require skilled individuals who can explain their value in a way that justifies a high price.

No matter how great a product is, or how wonderful the pricing or amazing the service might be, nothing can happen until one person gets another person interested in taking action. Imagine you had designed the world's fastest car, coded the most amazing app, or even invented a life-saving medical device. If no customers ever found out about it, then it wouldn't have made the slightest difference to your life... or anyone else's. The buyers who needed your product would never find it and you would go on wishing you could get rich.

The analogy to *MyCo* and your personal job search is probably obvious. I know you have amazing talents and work ethic, and so do you. But until someone who can actually give you a job begins to understand why you are different and better than all the other resume-carrying candidates out there, it doesn't matter. The situation doesn't improve until you begin getting paid.

Those are good reminders for the beginning of this chapter because it's time to move past theory and exercises. This is where the rubber meets the road and we get really busy!

To sell yourself to employers, you're going to simply continue on your personal sales journey toward its logical conclusion:

- You have already figured out who you are and what you want (your model).
- You also have a very clear portrait of the Ideal Prospect.
- You just learned how to prospect – with three concrete methods.
- As you apply the three methods, you will generate 20 Ideal Prospects.
- You will learn in the coming chapters that the only thing you are truly selling is the meeting itself.
- And finally, you're going to turn these meetings into opportunities.

That isn't too complicated, is it? It's essentially the same process I followed when I was earning awards as a commission-only salesperson.

Back then I knew I had to work with my strengths if my young family was going to eat. So, even though other agents in the company would contact hundreds of potential clients per month in the hopes of finding a few buyers, I did things differently. The idea of reaching out to strangers and offering them insurance policies they hadn't shown any interest in felt uncomfortable to me. I worked for a great firm and believed in what I was selling, but didn't think hitting up an endless parade of strangers for money would be a good fit for my personality.

So, while my peers were busy knocking on doors and making cold calls over the phone, I used the three methods for finding leads that I've already explained.

First, I went down to the library and did some research. That gave me a starting point to work from.

Then, I kept my ear to the ground. For instance, I was in a public bathroom and noticed that the manufacturer of the touchless hand dryer was a local, western Massachusetts company. I wrote a letter, met the owner, and sold him a policy. Observation can work!

Most importantly, I used my third technique to build a comprehensive list of the people I knew who trusted me. It included friends, their parents, colleagues, professors, and so on. I started reaching out to that network to tell them about my work, and also to ask whom they could introduce me to. With those names in hand, I sent letters beginning with "I am writing at the suggestion of my good friend [friend's name]." I would then describe the "model" I was looking for. (Sample letters can be found in the appendix.) I soon reached 20 names. As I've already mentioned, all three techniques were valuable but I quickly learned that this method of finding Referred Leads was where I was earning the greatest number of solid opportunities for new sales.

In any case, over time I discovered a very predictable set of ratios were at work. For every ten people I reached out to, roughly seven would agree to meet with me. Of those seven people, one would usually turn into a new client. Once I understood this process, and the math behind it, it became easy to meet (and then exceed) my monthly sales quotas.

The same kind of math can work for you. By exploring a certain number of potential employers or openings, you virtually guarantee you will unlock some good career opportunities.

Making the Numbers Work

You might be thinking your sales skills aren't quite as sharp as mine, or that you have a personality type that makes it harder for you to reach out to employers. Those are both fair points, but I can almost guarantee the steps I have taught will work for you anyway. That's partly because I have seen it pay dividends again and again. It's also because you have some advantages I didn't.

The first advantage is that you only need to make a single "sale." I had to write multiple insurance policies every month if I wanted to keep living indoors. You just have to find *one* job to stay fed and clothed. That tilts the math heavily in your favor.

The other big advantage you have is that the people in your life are going to be eager to help you. We all like to see our friends, relatives, and students succeed, especially when they are doing something ambitious like searching for employment. Your contacts will be ready to assist if they can. That certainly wasn't the case for me. No one roots for a life insurance agent, unless they happen to be married to them. You are probably going to get a lot more help than I did.

What does all this mean? In doing this sort of thing for myself and with coaching clients over the years, I have found one simple piece of math holds up again and again. Basically, it boils down to this: *if you are able to generate 20 of these Ideal Prospect meetings your search is OVER*. In fact, most of you will be able to generate at least two job offers with just 14-15 appointments.

Do the math: 20 Ideal Prospects = 14 Meetings = 2 Career Offers. Internalize those numbers because they change everything!

This might seem unbelievable to you, particularly if you've been dredging through the standard "see job listings and send resumes" grind for months. What makes my approach so much different is that it relies on natural rapport. If you come face-to-face (or webcam-to-webcam) with enough of the right people, you are going to gel with at least one of them. That first meeting will feel very natural, to the point that the other person will take an interest in your career.

Most of you reading this book haven't had that kind of meeting or interview before. And really, that's the point. When someone is meeting you in a traditional job interview setting, everything is stacked against you. The interviewer can barely tell you from the other applicants and knows you might say just about *anything* to start getting a paycheck. Your side of the conversation isn't any easier because you only have a few minutes to answer a handful of stock questions in a way that separates you from the pack.

With a more personal selling approach we are skipping all of that. Not only are we avoiding situations where you're put on the spot answering silly questions, but we are also dialing down the pressure even more by relying on predictable math. If one opportunity doesn't pan out, it's no big deal because you know others will.

Everything gets easier when you take the fear and stress out of job searching. Put the numbers and process in your favor and you might be amazed at what can happen... and how quickly things change for you.

Haley's Story:

After Tim coached me through some exercises designed to help me understand who I could become in my career, we began talking about the hidden job market. He explained to me that looking through job list-

ings was usually the least efficient way to get noticed by employers. This was a real eye-opener for me.

As we wrapped things up, he and I promised to stay in touch. It was early summer and rather than feeling lost or confused, I finally felt like I was ready to take the step forward with confidence.

Even in my excitement, I figured it would take a long time to find the right next step. But in September, just a few months later, I started at a new job. I found this new position through Tim's "referred lead prospecting" process. It actually turned out that the first person I met with offered me a job! I was going to assist with the recruiting and onboarding department at an up-and-coming technology company. The job had virtually everything I had identified on my list of wants: it was a fast-paced position, the office was in a trendy part of town, and the pay was great.

But most of all the new job was exciting. It meant meeting with new and potential hires from around the world. I got to travel, and to entertain guests from all kinds of different countries. When I wasn't running training and information sessions, I was taking colleagues out for drinks or meeting with senior managers. For someone who had been in school just a couple of years ago it was a dream come true. And then, once again, things changed.

17

SELL LIKE A CACTUS

I f you walk miles over a baked patch of earth, through a winding trail under the hot Arizona sun, you can find the world's wisest advisor. For decades he has fielded questions about marriages and mergers, investments and startup concepts. Through blazing afternoons and bitter cold evenings he waits for newcomers to arrive with the questions and worries that have been keeping them up at night.

The hermit I'm talking about never speaks, and he wears the same uncomfortable robe every day. But the most surprising thing about him is that he isn't a shaman, a spirit guide, or even a desert healer... he's a cactus who lives at the 17th hole of a popular golf course.

This cactus sits silently. He absorbs every word and gesture directed to him as one weary golfer after another comes to explain their problems or dilemmas. Those who have troubles on their mind go out to stretch their legs, distract themselves with a silly game, and then unburden themselves to the world's ultimate listener. In the process they find a fresh point of view, along with answers that seemed hidden before they started speaking.

Does this sound silly? Maybe it is. I made the cactus up as a way to explain an important concept to a client of mine years ago. I wanted him to understand that real communication, and especially *letting someone be heard*, is the key to finding answers and resolving conflicts.

I maintain that a spiky plant could heal marriages, settle partnership disputes, and give silent advice that would lead to career breakthroughs. I know this because coaches like myself have been able to do the same for decades (or maybe centuries) by simply *listening*.

There are many, many problems in this world that can be solved – or at least made less intense – by having someone to talk to. When you understand that principle and its power, you become a better friend, a more effective leader, and a stronger salesperson.

This leads us back to the approach I used to sell so many life insurance policies... and the simple playbook you can follow to generate more career opportunities.

It is now time to talk about the meetings you are going to have with your Ideal Prospects. I want to educate you about the sale of an intangible. Then, I want to apply a few selling "rules" to the challenge of finding and closing a deal. It's all about forgetting what you used to know about interviewing and aligning the product you have to sell – *you* – to your IP's true wants and needs.

Let's get started on key points of Consultative Selling:

The Consultative Selling Approach

The definition of consultative selling is that people, in the final analysis, do *not* buy because they understand a product (vis-à-vis all the products in a certain space). We would like to think that buying (and by extension, selling) is based on logic and the best product always wins. *Wrongo!* No, the sales process is much more emotional and based on "gut." People don't buy because they understand why a specific choice is the best one; instead, *they buy because they think that the salesperson understands them and their problems.*

This reality means that, as you are both the CEO of *MyCo* and also its only product, you are in an interesting position. In a job interview the interviewer will only buy if their gut is telling them that you understood them and their problems better than any other candidate they've met. Your job isn't to position yourself as the best product. You just have to show you understand their needs.

Does this run contrary to most of the advice you have received in the past? Maybe, but that's why it works. Once, when I was selling insurance, I actually sold a product I had never heard of. It happened because I had built so much trust with a potential client that he started talking extensively about what he really needed. I carefully documented everything he said, brought it to the advanced underwriting attorneys at my company, and let them identify the right set of insurance policies to meet his needs. He bought everything. Not because I dazzled him with my sales pitch, but because I *listened* carefully to him.

This may be the most important lesson of this book. The central Timbo belief, gleaned from coaching thousands of people through many decades, is that people have a *Universal Need to Be Understood.* If we can hold back from talking and "pitching stuff" (for example, about how much we need a job) and just LISTEN, the prospect feels understood. *Bingo!*

Listening carefully and with an open mind builds *huge* trust in sales. There is no need for fancy "closing lines" when you have done an awesome "opening" job of listening. Please don't forget this one!

Also realize you need to have the patience to listen to all of it. It is hard to hold back and hear another person's whole saga before responding. But it's entirely necessary. After you have listened to their song, you have built up some real trust. The other person feels understood. This gives you the right to float a different interpretation of what their real problems are.

This bit of insight is gold. You can't recommend solutions to a problem until another person feels confident you understand it. In 35+ years, I have run across many people who are unable to accurately represent their critical issues. It is simply too close to them, too personal, too emotional to get it right. Often, they need to voice their ideas out loud before they can move past the current roadblock.

The people I work with are smart people. If they had their problems framed properly they would have solved them long ago. But they never make it to that point before working with me. If I listen to their stated problem clearly, it builds trust in the process. Then I have earned the right to ask follow-up questions that lead to a solution I want to provide.

You may be thinking that you are too young or inexperienced to help the person you are speaking with identify issues they haven't thought of, but you aren't. If you listen carefully, as an objective person, you will shock yourself at what you can figure out.

Your job in an interview isn't to sell by telling. Instead, I want you to ask smart questions like: "You did a nice job describing your central issues. If I'm understanding correctly, you have these three problems (state them)." Assuming you're on target, you can then ask something along the lines of: "Would you be open to a slightly different interpretation of the problem set?"

In practical terms, people sense when another person is trying to take them where they don't want to go in a conversation. The only successful approach to persuasion is to help someone realize their own self-interest is aligned with yours. They have to FEEL (yes, feel, not think) that you understand their needs without any sense you are in the conversation to meet your own needs.

My last piece of advice is to leave any distractions at home. It can be tempting to show up at an interview or meeting with "stuff" you can show an employer. Inexperienced salespeople do this all the time. Even if they have taken an entire day with me on consultative sales training, when they get to the meeting, the last thing they want to enter into is a dialogue that is a true back-and-forth, unscripted discussion.

To fight this, I tell my trainees that the only weapon they are allowed to take into the first meeting is an empty yellow pad of paper. That's all. "Can it be white paper?" I have been asked. While yellow or white doesn't matter a hoot to me, *an empty pad is everything*. You cannot go into a meeting carrying a big briefcase loaded down with products and charts and other goodies that are meant to distract or tell the other person about you. Put them away. Listen. Take notes. Begin to organize the high-level design of the client problems. That is what a gifted salesperson does, and it's what will help you find the job you're looking for.

Ask and Receive

In order for your listening approach to be successful, you need to ask good questions. In fact, you'll often have to ask three or four of them in a series to get to a real answer that scratches below the surface. It's when a contact or employers tells you something you couldn't have gotten from a website that you've struck gold.

For a sense of what I mean, consider this conversation:

"Would you be comfortable telling me what you typically look for when you're hiring someone?"

"We don't really pay attention to GPAs or test scores. I like to see that someone has played sports or been involved in a club."

"I haven't heard that before. Could you tell me why?"

"Because anyone can learn the technical, day-to-day side of the job. What we really need are people who are mentally resilient and will stick with the job and be part of the team when we are going through a busy period. It's about toughness and consistency more than brains."

Think of the advantage you would have with this little piece of inside information. Now imagine how many of these insights you could get through 20 or 30 minutes of face-to-face time with someone who had the power to hire you or had made similar hiring decisions in the past. Hopefully this short example illustrates the need for good questioning skills.

Consultative Selling and Your Job Search

Once you know how to use the power of consultative selling, navigating the jungle we call a job interview gets easier. That's a good thing, because the typical ask-and-answer format associated with the hiring process doesn't work very well.

It's not hard to figure out why. The interviews young people are going to do today aren't much different than the ones I was sitting through 40 years ago. The format almost always goes something like this:

- First, you shake hands (at least pre-Covid you did) and go into an interview room.
- Next, there is an awkward small talk period designed to make the transition toward the actual interview easier (spoiler alert: it usually doesn't).
- The first question sounds like, "Please tell me a little about yourself," or "Can you please run me through your background?"
- The next question is along the lines of "What are your strengths? What are your weaknesses?"
- The third question will be something like, "Where do you see yourself three to five years from now?"
- And finally, the interviewer will likely ask, "Do you have any questions yourself?"

Now, because I know my readers are sharp, I'm sure many will have sensed a problem here. Given what you now know about consultative selling, does this sequence of events raise any issues or red flags? Do you feel any alarm bells going off?

If you got a sense of danger while thinking about the generic job interview, then give yourself a gold star. What was described breaks just about *every one* of Uncle Timbo's rules. The distinct crumbling sound you hear in the back of your mind is the echo of this opportunity blowing up on the horizon. That burnt rubber smell is your future going up in smoke.

Do you see the problems? Each of these questions, starting with the first one, is set up in a way to invite you to talk about *your* 94%. The interviewer is asking you to describe yourself as the solution to a problem you don't know anything about yet. The subsequent questions all follow suit.

That's not consistent with the consultative selling framework. It doesn't make you stand out in the interviewer's mind, either.

A better approach is to make sure *you* are the one who transitions from small talk to business talk. You simply wait until the introductory portion of the meeting seems to be winding down and then ask a question. Or you could even wait until the interviewer asks you to describe yourself and turn the conversation around. You could phrase it in a way that sounds something like this:

"Before we get started, I would be very interested in hearing about how long you've been here, and maybe what you look for in new hires."

Some young people are hesitant to try to set the direction for an interaction in this way. If you're one of them, remember that you actually have a bit of power, and probably more than you realize. Executives are very, very interested in getting the right type of young talent in their company. If you can keep the focus of the conversation on the interviewer's 94% – specifically, what does and doesn't work in their company or department – then you will be following the consultative selling framework and establishing trust. Also, you will be learning all about what they look for in a new recruit. Then, you can answer their questions with details and anecdotes that align perfectly with the situation.

A job interview can give you a wonderful opportunity to establish rapport with someone who could hire you, and to stand out from the competition. To achieve these outcomes, though, you need to master the art of turning the interview into more of a dialogue than a one-sided conversation.

You *have* to have the other person engaged in talking. Otherwise, the interviewer is going to ask you the deadly questions I've outlined above. Then, you'll be forced to start talking about yourself... just like all the other applicants do. At that point it's only a matter of seconds before the interviewer zones out and goes back to thinking about their 94% – their own job and its struggles, something their spouse said that morning, the trouble they were having with their kids, planning a vacation, etc.

Don't fall into that trap. You have the tools and skills to do better.

18

YOU'RE LOOKING FOR, NOT ASKING FOR, A JOB

There are many positives to reading a book. For instance, you can move through material at your own pace, revisiting as needed. That's convenient for both of us. You might be reading this chapter at 2 am right now, while I can be sleeping soundly in my bed. And of course, I can share what I've learned over the course of several decades with thousands of you without enduring an endless loop of flights, drives, or online calls.

The downside, though, is that I can't check on you... at least not in the traditional sense. So let me ask now: *how are you doing?*

Learning a whole new approach to selling and career development can be energizing and stressful all at once. No matter which of these you're feeling most, I have some good news for you. If you have followed along and actually done the work, then the hard part is over. It might not *feel* that way, but you are much farther along the job search process than you realize.

How can I say that? It's easy. You have done something most people never do by evaluating your own strengths and weaknesses. Then you thought about the direction you wanted your career to take and have identified contacts who can lead you to the next step. You have even learned about consultative selling. The math is almost guaranteed to work out in your favor. The only thing left to do is physically put yourself in the meetings we've been talking about.

Asking for the Meeting

I have mentioned in previous chapters that the only thing you are selling to anyone is a meeting. I would be surprised if this comment hasn't led to some confusion and raised eyebrows. Yet, this notion will be key to your success in your "sales calls" with your Ideal Prospects.

I know almost everyone reading this book does not want to be a salesperson. I understand that. That is why it's so important to understand what you are selling. As you begin to approach Ideal Prospects you are NOT attempting to get them to hire you for a job. Why would you? They might not have anything available. For you to try to get hired when there are no openings would be unproductive, and possibly irritating.

So, instead of asking for a job, you're just selling them on the idea of spending a little time with you. Then, the rest will take care of itself.

Let me explain. Once you have secured 20 Ideal Prospects you should not be concerned with whether they have a need. What you *should* know is how each one seems to fit the profile of your model. You also know that if there *were* a job you have a huge edge because you were referred to them by someone they know.

No one wants to interview a young person they have no need to hire. But most of your Ideal Prospects will be happy to meet with you and give some advice. From there, you can create your opening based on the math I outlined earlier.

I'm going to explain this process, of course, but for the moment let's keep it short and sweet: sell as many of your 20 Ideal Prospects as possible on the idea of meeting with you for 30 minutes or more. It's not a lot to ask, of you or your IP, but nothing happens until you have secured a meeting.

Job Hunting Is a Contact Sport

How do you actually reach out to your IPs? That's up to you. You can write them (see the sample letter in the appendix). Or you can call them. You could even use email or social media. But when you are in touch with them, here is the simple song you want to sing:

"Hi, I'm writing at the referral of Sofia Doe, our mutual friend. I am conducting a unique campaign in that I have defined what I want (my ideal job) and shared this model with close contacts of mine. One of these was Sofia, who suggested I contact you. I would like to spend 30 minutes with you and learn about your company and tell you a little about me. Thanks so much for giving me the time."

There can only be three objections to having a meeting with you:

1. They have no job openings.
2. They have no time.
3. They have no interest.

The first two objections are simple to overcome, but the third is rare because you are coming from a CI.

Let's start with the easy ones. For the first two objections, you want to be clear that you have no expectation that your IP has a job available. Rather, your referral source said that they have a very interesting background and you simply want to learn more about them, their company, and the industry to continue to inform your job search. And, you also want to be clear that you're happy just taking half an hour of their time if that's all they can spare. Be flexible about the when and where of the matter and they'll likely agree.

For the third objection, there are some people who are difficult to meet in this way. If you absolutely can't break through the brick wall, one option is to use guilt and ask if there is someone else they would recommend to speak with you. After all, you are trying to learn about the company and the industry. Even if a particular IP won't see you, they might be willing to refer you elsewhere. It is a compliment to ask, "Could you possibly recommend someone yourself?"

To connect a few dots for you, think about the process of using Referred Leads to find your Ideal Prospects. It will help those contacts refer you once they understand that you won't actually be pressuring someone to give you a job. If you are sincere and confident about selling the meeting and nothing more, then your mature approach will come through. It then becomes very easy for them to refer you to a contact of theirs.

I know it's not easy looking for a job, but I also want you to understand this process is very doable. You *will* be successful with the methods I've outlined. With your newfound knowledge of how easy it becomes to make new contacts when you just sell a meeting, I'm going to restate some of what you have learned about networking. Your goal is to become a detective. You are trying to find out who might be in a position to help you reach the next stage of your career. Then you want to discover how you can best make a connection with them.

Naturally, this is an area where tools like LinkedIn can be a huge help. On the one hand, you can use them to research contacts and get to know them directly. And on the other hand, you can begin to grow your network by connecting with recent graduates from your school and department, or others who know you personally, so you can build these bridges for the future.

This kind of networking can take a bit of time and follow-up, but it's worth the effort. Agreements of any kind – from hiring decisions to billion-dollar mergers – are often built on relationships. Having your Centers of Influence reach out to those who can create opportunities for you allows for warmer introductions. An executive or division manager, for example, is highly likely to meet with you if they get your name from someone they know or trust. You can always introduce yourself if there isn't any other option, but I recommend you try doing things the easy way first.

Most people who are established in their careers really *do* want to help young people who are looking to follow in their footsteps. But they also have to protect their own time and mental health. They may worry that, by agreeing to meet with you, they will be giving up an entire day. Or, they could be afraid you'll be clingy and beg for a job. Who would sign up for that?

Your prospect might also worry they won't know how to interact with you. Believe me, once you get past a certain number of birthdays you are very aware of not being "with it" in the eyes of someone who still knows what kind of music is popular!

To conquer these fears make it abundantly clear that you only want half an hour of your Ideal Prospect's time. Let them know you aren't asking for anything more and that the purpose of the meeting will be for you to gather information about the kind of work you want to do. This is an easy thing for someone to say "yes" to.

As a salesperson, I would have gone hungry if I had tried to get new potential clients to spend hours with me so I could tell them about everything I had to sell. No one has that kind of time and even if they did that wouldn't be an enjoyable way to spend it. So, I had to settle for borrowing their attention in short increments, knowing I would be granted more time in the future if I handled these short meetings the right way.

A half-hour meeting works because it's an easy thing to ask for and agree to. In the next chapter I'm going to teach you how to make every second of that interaction count.

Approach to the Ideal Prospect

By now, you have done all the hard work. It is almost game time. You have followed Timbo's building blocks for landing your next job. You now have to create as many meetings as you can with all the Ideal Prospects you have generated. How should you approach each one in a way that best enhances your chances of securing your meeting?

One way is to actually have your Center of Influence place a call to the Ideal Prospect they suggested you meet. After all, your CI knows this person, so it should be easy for this person to arrange the meeting for you. That makes sense, but I'll stick with my earlier warning: if at all possible schedule these appointments on your own. Otherwise, you face risks that are largely out of your control. One is that time goes by and your CI simply forgets to make the introduction. Or, wires got crossed around dates, times, or locations. Even worse, it could turn out your CI isn't very good at making these calls and fails.

Why not put the odds in your favor and just take on the responsibility yourself? You can be sure it gets done, while also positioning yourself as a young professional that others want to help.

So, assuming you're going to take control and contact your Ideal Prospect directly, how should you do it? You could place a call. You would mention that you were referred by your CI who "suggested that you would be a good person for me to briefly chat with as I look for a career opportunity." That might work, but you can get a little pushback simply because your IP was not prepared. Your call might have caught them off guard. Also, there is a chance you could fumble your words on the phone.

With the right script (you can steal freely from the sample introduction letter I have provided in the appendix) and a calm demeanor you might be able to make a phone call work. I still think the odds are against you, though, so I'm going to suggest something more low-key.

You could also approach your Ideal Prospect by dropping in on them at their place of work. This tactic is tied to the observation method of prospecting I referenced in Chapter 14. Please go back and search out the example of the fellow who was looking for a job in the construction business and approached a hard hat worker on a job site with the name of a company plastered all over the place. In certain circumstances, the drop-in can be very effective.

The practice that has always worked best for me was to write letters to my Ideal Prospects. I have included some examples of letters that have worked for younger folks in the appendix. Feel free to borrow, steal, copy, or amend them as you like.

In essence, your letter should revolve around three key points:

The first paragraph lets the IP know you are writing at the suggestion of your CI who recommended the two of you get together.

Your second paragraph explains you are conducting a rather unique campaign in that you have built a model of what you want in a job and discussed these goals with your close friends and acquaintances. One of these was your friend, John Doe.

The third paragraph should make it clear you are not approaching the meetings you have created with the idea that any one of them had a specific job opening. Rather, you are just looking to get together with someone who has more knowledge than you and can help fill in the gaps in your knowledge.

Don't feel or pass on too much pressure in these letters. You should be very relaxed since you are only looking to create meetings tied to your now fervent belief that having a large number of Ideal Prospects will swing things your way.

And finally, are you looking for one more method for generating appointments, or have an Ideal Prospect you just can't reach through referrals? Let's please not forget the old-time method of firing out resumes rather randomly. This is not the rifle shot approach I have been teaching you, but it's true that shotguns sometimes hit random targets.

You can adapt the letter I outlined above to contact an IP out of the blue. Just mention why you think this person can help you in your search instead of naming a CI who introduced you if you don't have one. Believe it or not, I have sent many of these letters over the years and have gotten many responses from contacts I had never met, even when they were outside of my network.

Of course, the real secret isn't in using any one of these strategies – it's in being politely persistent. If the first commandment of Timbo selling is to know who you are and what you want, then the second is that you *must* generate meetings with Ideal Prospects. If you don't then your plan won't go anywhere.

19

IT'S TIME FOR YOU TO MEET YOUR IDEAL PROSPECT

I t probably won't take all that long for the *MyCo* sales plan to generate some leads. You might have a first meeting (or even several) set up within a couple of weeks. Now comes the moment of truth: it's time to take all that you have learned to this point and turn it into a job opportunity.

As we covered earlier, the best way to do this is *not* by talking about your skills, your ambitions, or even what you can do for a potential employer. Remember, we are following a consultative selling framework; we understand that other people will tell us what they want and need if we will only be willing to give them the time and space to do so. Knowing that, we are going to maximize the 30 minutes we have asked for by learning as much as we can from this person. Then, at the end of the meeting, we can figure out the best way forward.

Much of the success or failure of your meeting will be determined before you have ever said a word. That's because factors like your mindset, the environment, and your preparation can all impact the flow of conversation. When you get those elements right you feel confident and relaxed. Make mistakes, though, and you could find yourself rushed, on edge, or feeling defensive. I'm going to help you cover the most important bases.

And why not? To repeat our motto one more time, you know who you are, what you're good at, and what kind of job you are trying to find. You are about to learn the last piece of the puzzle that brings everything together.

Before Your Meeting

I want you to think of yourself as being in an important business meeting from the moment you leave your home. That means arriving at your destination early and treating the people around you with professionalism and respect. You would be amazed at how many interviews and introductions have gone south because a job seeker couldn't stop themselves from snapping at a receptionist or behaving badly toward a service worker. You must settle yourself and be at peace with your own 94%.

You might find it helpful to stay with thoughts about how you are prepared, that you know how to interview, and that you have conquered your fears because you are in control. By the time you arrive you should be exuding confidence and a real passion for your job search.

Your Powerful Meeting Strategy

By the time you're actually sitting down to meet your Ideal Prospect all the hardest work is done. Now you just have to let them tell about their past, the current state of their business or industry, and (very possibly) your future.

Remember, your goal is to be almost like the cactus, which never talks but always listens. As you go through the initial small talk portion of the meeting during the first few minutes, look for an opportunity to ask a few questions that will get the prospect speaking. You want them to be speaking about their 94% rather than you talking about your 94%. Get this right and you'll eventually get to your story.

As you move away from small talk, the idea is to get the conversation moving. The best way to do that is by asking focused questions. What kinds of questions might you ask during the initial meeting? Here are some you might begin with:

- "How did you get started on your career, or in this industry?"
- "What do you like about working in this business? What don't you like?"
- "What are some things you wish you would have known early on?"
- "Where do you see the industry or profession going in the next decade?"
- "What makes someone successful in this company or line of work? Are there certain traits or personality types that fit better than others?"
- "If you were in my shoes what would you be doing today to make yourself more marketable?"
- "I assume at some point in time you had to get your first job. How did you break in with no experience?

You of course would never ask all of these questions in order. Rather, you are having a back-and-forth conversation and these are potential ways to introduce topics.

Your Ideal Prospect's answer to any of these questions might result in you asking for further clarification or about a closely related topic. That allows you to create a back-and-forth conversation that opens them up. The IP is engaged versus daydreaming. At the same time, you are learning more and more about the company, its culture, the future of the organization or industry, and even what makes an employee the right fit. Your questions build trust with your prospect because the interchange is real. Trust is building.

If the meeting is going well enough, or if you use your consultative selling framework in the right way, you'll begin to notice a momentum shift.

Taking the Marbles of Power

Young people often feel like they have no power when meeting with potential employers. This can be a worry during meetings with Ideal Prospects, but also in situations that are set up as a "formal job interview." They sense they are in a position where they have all the desire and motivation to achieve an outcome (a job) while the other part doesn't care whether they get it or not.

That's not necessarily the case.

If you think about it, there are dozens of reasons someone might really need help in their business or department. Perhaps an employee has left recently and important tasks aren't being completed. Maybe a supervisor has two or three people working extra hours to cover the job, or are doing it themselves even though they don't have the time. Perhaps they just need someone with different skills, or a fresh perspective, to help them meet quarterly goals or carry their vision forward.

The point is even your Ideal Prospects have things they want out of meeting with referrals, as well. They just don't know which candidate – if any – can provide the help they need.

By understanding that, you can gradually tilt the power dynamic in any meeting you have with an IP in your favor. To help you understand how, I want you to imagine shiny red marbles that are on the table when you sit with a potential employer. Each one represents a little piece of control over the situation.

At the beginning of a meeting or interview, the person you are visiting with *does* have all the marbles. They have the information you want, and can open or close the gate to their company (along with any potential jobs within it). Other than being a bright and exciting young person, you don't have a lot to offer *in that first moment.*

That can change pretty quickly, though. As your meeting or interview progresses, you can use your consultative selling approach to show your IP that you aren't just looking for a paycheck. They can see you have a real curiosity about them and their business. Each question you ask keeps them thinking about their 94% rather than having to worry about yours. The trust and rapport that are created naturally lead them to value you more highly. Some of the marbles shift over to your side of the table.

As the conversation continues, and they can see that you are focused and mature enough to have considered your future career path, your IP may begin to wonder how you could help them reach *their* goals. By listening and not "pitching" yourself, you have put yourself in a position to be considered as a potential employee. Ironic, isn't it? More and more marbles are coming your way.

By the end of the meeting you may have gathered enough marbles that your Ideal Prospect is actually trying to *sell you* on the prospect of working with them. At the very least they could be open to a discussion along those lines. Don't worry, I'm going to show you how to stoke and nurture this interest in the next chapter.

For the moment, I just want you to recognize that while your red power marbles might not be real in the literal sense, they do very much affect your job search. As humans we tend to be ruled by fear and greed. Your Ideal Prospect may go into your meeting being fearful – fearful that you will badger them for a job, or talk endlessly about how smart you are. When you don't do these things, and instead engage their 94%, you appeal to their sense of greed. Specifically, you get them thinking, "I loved meeting with this young person and would hate to lose them to another company." Greed sells. Just ask any cactus.

20

TURNING INTRODUCTIONS INTO OPPORTUNITIES

How do you turn a quick first meeting with your Ideal Prospect into a potential career opportunity? It's simple. So simple, in fact, that it's almost easy to miss.

In the movies, slick sales professionals "go for the close" by tricking their clients with a complicated display of verbal jujitsu. In the real world, making a sale is usually more straightforward. And if you're using the Timbo-branded consultative selling system for job seekers, it's more natural. Let's review why this is.

You have assessed your own strengths and wants, creating a model of your intended career in the process. Then, you generated 10 to 15 meetings with Ideal Prospects who all represent potential opportunities. The odds seemed stacked against you: none of these people have indicated they were looking to hire a new person, and your IPs were holding all the marbles when you met. But then, following your consultative selling approach, you gained their trust and interest. The magic has happened. The marbles started to move to your side of the table.

Unearthing the Potential Opportunity

You may remember that the whole basis of the consultative selling method is to find someone who might need your help and learn more about them and the challenges they are facing. Then, if there is a good fit on both sides, you offer a solution.

How do you move into the phase of the appointment that gets down to brass tacks? And what is the next natural question?

Remember, we want things to feel as easy and natural as possible. So, you might say something to your IP like: "I appreciate all the time and information you have given me today. It seems to me, from my point of view, that we have talked about a potential viable path for me at your company. If you agree, I'd like to share with you the written document that illustrates what I'm looking for in my job search."

At this point you produce the model that you built outlining your next career move and the reasons it makes sense for you. This model will have to fit with what you just told the IP, namely, that this company and area of the company are what you are looking for.

Having this model is important for two reasons. First, it keeps you centered on what you're looking for. And second, when your interviewer sees you take it out they have proof that you came to the meeting knowing what you're after. They can see you aren't just making things up on the fly, or looking for the first job that comes around.

That creates a pair of positive outcomes for you. On the one hand, it makes your interest more specific. Remember earlier, when I mentioned that most people will have trouble thinking of referrals unless you give them specific prompts? The same thing is happening here. You are telling your IP exactly what you want and making it easier for them to offer suggestions to help you reach it.

At the same time, you are also giving them a more concrete idea of who you are as a "product" of sorts. This is critical because you suddenly become a solution to the issues and challenges they have discussed during your meeting – a.k.a. the problems and goals that make up their 94%.

Most organizations turn over employees at a rate that makes it a constant challenge to bring new people in fast enough. It is especially difficult to find bright people who intend to stick around. That means your IP might begin thinking of you for jobs that have either recently become open or might become vacant in the near future. They could even consider inventing a role for you if they think you could be a valuable asset to their team. It happens!

Can you feel the rest of the marbles sliding over to you? Get this transition to your job search model right and it will happen quite naturally.

Before we move on, however, I have to point out that you might not even reach this stage in the conversation on your own. Most of us never run across a good listener in our day-to-day lives. That's certainly true when we get together with someone – like a salesperson, for instance, or a job seeker – who wants something from us. They talk and talk, always thinking about what they need and never focusing on what they can offer. When you put your consultative selling skills to good use you separate yourself from all the other potential employees out there. You suddenly become an invaluable quantity: *someone who gets it.*

Because of this, there is a high probability that your IP will raise the topic of employment with their organization, or someone they know, before you ever have to raise the subject.

Unfortunately, this usually isn't the end of the story. While it's possible you could leave a lunch meeting with your Ideal Prospect with a job offer in hand, most of the time there will be other hurdles to get over. It might be that your IP wants you to meet another owner or department head. Perhaps there are HR team members who have to be involved, or legal hiring guidelines to follow. They may just want you to sit for a more "official" job interview.

All of these outcomes are fine. You're skating toward an empty net, miles ahead of other potential employees who don't know there is a job in the first place and haven't built up the same level of trust and rapport with your IP. I'm going to show you how to finish things and get the job in the next chapter, but know now that it's (naturally) just the simple extension of everything you have done to this point. There's not much to stress about.

Before we address that we have to consider one other possibility...

What if There Really Is No Opening?

I'm firmly convinced, as I've mentioned several times, that you only need 10-15 Ideal Prospect meetings to generate at least one or two solid job offers. However, that also means that several of your meetings *won't* result in immediate interest or referrals. How should you handle things then?

Don't make the mistake of thinking that all is lost if your meeting isn't a raging success. There are many reasons you could find yourself in such a situation. Perhaps your IP truly can't think of a job you'd be suited for, within their organization or another. It could be they have something in mind but need to check with another person first. Maybe they would like to hire you down the road and don't want to steer you toward a competitor.

All of these are possibilities. It's also true that personalities and styles don't always match. You just might not be a good fit to work together. Your IP might not like you that much, or vice versa. That's okay, too. It's the reason I want you to meet with more than a dozen Ideal Prospects and not one or two.

When you find that the conversation isn't as free-flowing as you might wish, or that your IP doesn't take much interest in your job search model, keep your consultative selling hat on. Be like a detective and just keep asking questions. You could say something like, "I hope you know this time has been very valuable for me. Do you mind if I ask whether you think it went well?"

At that point, you put your IP into the role of a mentor. They will likely give you some insights on your skill as a networker and interview. Make some notes because these can help you in future interactions. Even more importantly, they will likely suggest next steps. That could include passing along your resume, scheduling an additional appointment, or nudging you toward a different avenue in your job search. Again, any of these outcomes is a good one because they represent advice from someone who knows you at least a little bit and has industry knowledge. They may not become an employer, but they could still serve as a Center of Influence for you.

That might not be the perfect outcome you were hoping for, but it still helps you move forward. And even in the case of a terrible meeting you are gaining experience. Remember my interview with the rubber company? It was a train wreck, but I learned some things. Every bit of practice makes it easier to move ahead the next time.

After the Meeting

Regardless of the outcome, it's important to wrap up your meeting with an IP the right way. You should shake hands with the person, let them know that you appreciate what they have done for you, and go your separate ways. Just don't make the mistake of thinking this is where your work with that person ends.

Obviously, you may have agreed to take some next step, such as forwarding your resume or getting together for a follow-up meeting. But even in the absence of that kind of commitment there are other things you can do to improve your odds of ultimately ending up in a new job.

The first step is to make some notes while the interaction is still fresh in your mind. Did things go well, or could they have been better? Were you confident and relaxed, or did you tense up when asking questions? Did you get the sorts of details you are looking for? Were there unexpected insights? Were you able to close the meeting effectively and determine what your next moves should be?

These kinds of insights are extraordinarily valuable, so you'll want to jot them down as quickly as you can. You might even create a meeting or interview scorecard, like the one you made for job opportunities, that you can use to track your performance from one meeting to the next.

Another thing you want to do right away is make a written note of any activities you need to schedule or perform as a result of the meeting. For instance, if you promised to call another person at a certain time, jot this down. You don't want to ruin the impression the other person has of you because of simple disorganization or forgetfulness. As the old saying goes, the faintest ink is better than the strongest memory. Write down anything that is crucial for you to recall later, particularly dates, times, and locations.

Something that might seem old-fashioned to you is to take a few minutes to write a handwritten thank-you note after every meeting. In today's world, a handwritten note can really set you apart. You don't have to spend hours composing the perfect message. Just tell them you appreciated their time and will act on the advice you were given. So few people ever take the time to follow through with a simple step like this. It's incredibly old school, but that's why it sets you apart from all the other job seekers and young professionals your contact will meet. It's the kind of thing people remember about you.

And finally, you should make every meeting a chance to adjust or improve your sales approach. Ask yourself what (if anything) has changed as a result of the meeting. Do you need to add new contacts to your list, change your expectations for your next job, or make some other adjustment? It might take a bit of thought and reflection to come up with the answers, as well as some time spent with your Board of Directors. But given that the goal is to find the right opportunity, and not just the next paycheck, it's well worth the effort.

If you follow the consultative selling approach I have outlined you will quickly end up in a situation where you have additional meetings with IPs, formal employment interviews, or both. Luckily, these will be a lot easier and less stressful than they are for most people because of the relationship-building approach you have followed to this point. In the next chapter I'll show you how to take the final steps toward an actual job offer.

21

SURVIVING THE FORMAL JOB INTERVIEW

E ntire books and seminars have been put together on the subject of successfully navigating job interviews. Some of them are valuable, others less so. But mostly, I think they miss the point. That's because most of the hard work should be done long before you ever set foot in an interviewer's office.

If you have followed my advice, you will usually be facing what I would call a *friendly* interview environment. That means you've gotten a very warm introduction (or possibly even a quasi-offer for a job) from an Ideal Prospect who wants to work with you. At the very least, you have probably been referred by someone the interviewer knows, likes, and/or respects. That puts you in a very strong position. The interviewer will probably be expecting to hire you instead of seeing you as "just another person off the street."

That doesn't mean you can take it easy, though. I want you to be relaxed, but to stay vigilant. It isn't time to celebrate just yet.

On the other hand, you could be called for an interview from the traditional job search process. Maybe you were contacted by an employer after sending resumes (remember when I told you to keep doing that?). Or, maybe your network of referrals introduced you to someone, like a friend of a friend, who doesn't know you at all.

Obviously, in this situation the odds aren't quite as strongly in your favor. But they aren't impossible, either. After all, you've gotten yourself into the right room. If you've been following my advice then you are interviewing for a job you actually want. And now you have a real chance to get it.

Although I have described two very different scenarios, one warmer and one colder, your approach to the interview should be the same no matter how the opportunity appeared. You are going to continue with your consultative selling approach to make yourself stand out in the crowd.

Avoid the Job Interview Booby Traps

I know you are eager to hear secret interviewing and persuasion tips, but let me start by teaching you something a lot of job seekers don't realize: the interview starts *before* it formally begins.

To refresh your memory, you need to be on your best behavior when you arrive. Dress nicely in freshly washed and pressed clothes. Be sure you get to the interview location 10 or 15 minutes early. Be nice to any receptionists or other employees you meet. If you have a tendency to spill things, don't show up holding a giant cup of coffee.

None of this is groundbreaking, but it all matters. You would be amazed at how many candidates shoot themselves in the foot by displaying poor etiquette. Interviewers talk to the people around them. If you are rude, disheveled, or exhibiting signs that you'd rather be anywhere else in the world, then the person who makes a hiring decision is going to find out.

We have gone through several chapters of hard work, helping you build trust and connections. I don't want you to miss out on opportunities because you let your guard down now.

Also remember that preparation is your friend. You should scout your interviewer, their organization, and even the location of the interview before the meeting if possible. Practice sample questions and answers to common interview queries so you can handle them with ease. And, make a note of any questions you have about the position so you'll remember to ask them at the end.

These steps will give you a sense of confidence and keep you from missing important details.

Read the Room and Set the Tone

The first few minutes of your interview can be incredibly revealing. You might be meeting with one person, including your IP, or several people at once. Usually, the proceedings will start with a little bit of small talk.

Your first task, during these informal moments, is to get a sense of what the personal dynamics involved might be. You're not only trying to work out your rapport with the interviewer(s), but also their relationships with each other. Some of the people in the room probably won't know you. Likewise, you won't necessarily know what they have been told about you, or how they feel about the situation.

A best-case scenario would be that you have been recommended by a person who is both friendly with and respected by the interviewer. The interviewer may need, for whatever reason, to add their rubber stamp of approval to the hiring decision. But, they come into the interview wanting and expecting to like you. All that has to happen is that you assure them you are a relatively normal and productive person.

Those are great interview conditions, but things don't always work out so perfectly. That's true even when you have a recommendation or referral. It's also possible that your IP and the interviewer barely know each other. Maybe the IP's recommendation carries some weight, but isn't entirely persuasive. It could even happen that your interviewer wants to line up a job for their niece or nephew and you are in the way, or that they really don't like your IP and resent being told they need to meet with you.

Are any of these situations fair? No. Are they your fault? No. Do they happen in the real world? *Every day.*

Luckily, none of these worst-case hypotheticals has to bring your job search to a dead end. When you understand the subtext and stay focused on your interviewer's 94%, good things happen. With a little bit of effort you can get everyone involved on your side.

Sound impossible? It's not. Years ago I was putting together a deal with a leader in a large hospital. I followed a consultative selling approach (of course) and found out exactly what kind of help his team needed. Everything about our skills and their goals lined up perfectly. The budget was right in line with what the client had expected, as well. I remember thinking that I should take my wife somewhere sunny to celebrate this new piece of business that was going to benefit everyone.

When I proposed that we finalize the deal, however, I saw a storm cloud cross over my prospective client's face. I had to resist the urge to panic or start telling him about all the great things that would come from our work together. Instead, I took a guess and asked a simple question: "If we go ahead with this project, is there someone whose reaction you'll be worried about?"

The change in his expression told me I had hit the jackpot. With a little more questioning and encouragement I found out my potential client was quite intimidated by one of the other department heads who would be involved. The feeling was that they disliked and distrusted one another. Worst of all, there was no way for the deal to proceed without buy-in from both sides.

So, no deal right? Well, I asked my potential client if I could meet with the other department head and try to get to the bottom of things. He was hesitant but agreed. Upon meeting with the big and scary executive I found that he, in turn, was intimidated by the first department chair. The whole thing was a circle of misunderstanding that was easily sorted out with some careful questioning. In the end the project moved ahead, our work was a smashing success, and the two former rivals became great friends when the air had been cleared.

I don't want you to miss the point. This isn't a story about my sales prowess; it's about the power of observation and listening. If you are dialed in to your interviewer, and really staying attuned to their 94%, then you'll stand out to them just as you did your IP. Simply being attentive to what someone else is actually saying and thinking lets you turn around even the toughest situations. It's your superpower.

Turning the Interview Into a Two-Way Street

Do you remember what I told you in the last chapter? There is no secret sales closing technique. Neither is there a special handshake, power tie, or body language secret that will get you into the job you want.

So what *does* work? The same thing as always: understanding what someone wants and giving them the solution. That's the basic idea behind the consultative selling framework, and it's what melts (most of) the stress away from an interview setting.

If it's possible, make the transition away from small talk and toward a formal interview yourself. When you sense that everyone is comfortable in the room and ready to begin, kick things off by asking some questions. You can say things like:

"Before we begin, I was hoping you could tell me a little bit about how you got started with this organization?"

That gives the interviewer the chance to tell you a bit about their background. It also shifts things onto their 94%. You can then follow up with more questions. Here are a few examples:

- "What makes for a good candidate for this position?"
- "What kinds of people have been successful in this role before?"
- "How would you expect a person in this job to progress in their career?"

Now you're asking targeted questions that tell you about the other person's point of view – specifically, what they are looking for in a new hire. Remember, you can't give answers until you let someone explain their view of a problem. Don't fall into the mistake of using the interview to talk about every item on your resume, or how great you are.

To be fair, you are probably going to have to offer *some* information about yourself. Just like with your first appointment with an Ideal Prospect, a formal job interview can still be a give-and-take situation. The more you can keep the conversation moving, and especially coming back to the interviewer's needs when they make a hiring decision, the more marbles you're going to have.

You might be thinking this all sounds too easy. Well, it is. That's because you did all the hard work much earlier in the job search process. Now you're just seeing it through to its logical conclusion.

Early in this book I explained all the reasons that the so-called "basics" of finding a job don't work. However, none of those reasons hold up when you are interviewing for a position that you have been recommended for, and that you know suits your short- and long-term goals. It is like the difference between asking someone you don't know to buy an insurance policy from you versus recommending a very specific solution to someone who already knows they want insurance, likes you, and is aware of the cost. Selling is always simpler when you've reached this point the right way.

And, even if you do have to come in cold – without a recommendation or referral – you'll know how to interview in a way that sets you apart from the other candidates. Either way, if you make it to this stage in the process you are very likely to be offered a job if it truly is the right fit for you. So now you have to answer the next question, which is: *should you take it?*

22

RESPONDING TO JOB OFFERS

S o, you have followed my steps and exercises and a few weeks or months later someone has formally offered you a job. Congratulations! It's time to leave a five-star review for this book and put it away, right?

Well, *maybe*.

The goal of this whole process isn't to generate job offers (or at least that isn't the *only* goal). It's to put you in a role where you are comfortable, appreciated, and moving toward a future you feel good about. Having a job offer in hand gives you new possibilities, but accepting it also closes off other potential paths.

That doesn't mean you shouldn't take the job, of course, just that you have a lot to consider. I don't want you to rush ahead and get into a situation that isn't right for you. Instead, I want you to be guided by your deepest dreams and values. That makes this the perfect time to remind yourself of why you did all this work in the first place.

Revisiting Your Job Scorecard

You might be thinking to yourself that you would *gladly* accept any hypothetical job that's going to be offered to you, especially if you have taken the time to figure out what you want, met with a potential employer, and gone through the interview process. And you probably *will* take the job. I just don't want you to make a quick decision, especially if it means underselling your own abilities.

I want you to understand you will view things differently once you work this process earnestly. What you will learn is other people just like you get hired for jobs they love all the time. If you reach a point where you have several different irons in the fire you might be hesitant to commit to one right away. That can especially be true if you have additional meetings or opportunities coming right around the corner.

If you were doing sales as your profession, this wouldn't be a problem. I could write an insurance policy for one person on Monday and then issue two more on Tuesday. But when it comes to *MyCo*, sales have to be made very carefully. Once you accept a job, you will be taking yourself off the market. It is so hard to close on a career opportunity when you have three exciting meetings next week.

So, how do you decide whether to accept a job when you might have (or expect) other competing offers?

The first step is to take a deep breath, congratulate yourself on the work you've done to get to this point, and then remember that you don't have to make a snap decision. If the offer is in writing let it sit for a few hours. If your contact phones you to offer a job, thank them and ask if you can have a bit of time to think about things. They should understand that you might want some room to make a big call that will impact your life in numerous ways.

Then, ask yourself important questions like the following:

- Is there anything in the written job offer that surprises you? Is the compensation what you expected?
- Where would you be working, and who would be supervising you?
- What sort of future could you see for yourself in the next few years if you were to accept the job?
- Have you learned anything new about the position, yourself, or your career path by meeting with your contact or researching the job? Do the new facts change anything?

If these questions seem familiar to you, then congratulate yourself for paying attention. What we are essentially doing at this stage is going back to the scorecard you created earlier in the job search process and updating it with any new information.

If you recall, I wanted you to develop your scorecard so you could paint a clearer picture of your future. Now you can use the things you wrote down to consider whether they still accurately reflect your priorities. You can also refer back to your notes and be sure you aren't discarding anything that might affect your decision in the heat of the moment.

It's a big deal to be offered a job. The sense of achievement you feel, and the weight of the decision in front of you, can affect your emotions in ways that make it hard to separate euphoria and confusion from practical considerations. Having some written notes you can rely on can help you make the right call.

Another way to gain some clarity on your decision is by speaking with your Board of Directors. Let them know what you are facing and get their impressions. Ask them for their honest feedback. The decision about whether to accept a job or not will always be yours, but the advisors in your life can provide perspective when you need it most.

Beyond that, my advice would be to trust your gut and don't try to outsmart yourself. Having too many job opportunities is a nice problem. It allows you to be a little bit pickier than you might be otherwise. It's entirely possible that you will have ranked one position, supervisor, or opening above the others. If that's the case and you know what you want, then go after it. On the other hand, if your meetings and interviews lead you to discover that your priorities have changed, then don't be afraid to shift directions. This is all about your growth and fulfillment. You are the one who has to work in the job so act like the CEO of *MyCo* and make the best long-term decision.

Follow the Map You Left for Yourself

Look once again at your job scorecard. You can check out the appendix for other examples, too.

After you have studied them, ask yourself: what are your top 5-6 headlines? Have you prioritized them in the order of their importance? Your scorecard is a very helpful document. It brings logic to an emotional decision. Emotion is great at moving you to action, but you still need to think logically before jumping off the ledge (metaphorically) for a 50-foot drop into the ocean of a new career.

Follow these steps and you will come to a decision that feels right. You'll know you're making it based on what you wanted all along, not a momentary bout of euphoria or fear. When that moment arrives, formally accept the new job and then take some time to celebrate. By getting intentional about your career path and then working your way into the job that is on that path, you will have done something most people never will. That's worth feeling good about.

The only thing left after that is to start your new position and give it your all. If you have followed my advice you should be in a spot where you're excited to get up, go to work, and further your career. Enjoy that feeling and make the most of it.

Hopefully you will feel overjoyed and satisfied at this point. Just know that whether you pick the perfect job or sail off in what turns out to be the wrong direction, the journey won't end. You will likely change roles again at some point in the future. But the next time you need to make a career move you'll be that much more prepared.

23

JUMP!

J ob searches have a way of stretching on... and on and on. This is almost always due to the fact that the person who wants to make a career move puts off the hard work of prospecting – that is, building lists and reaching out to new contacts.

It's human nature to put off things that are hard. And make no mistake, putting yourself out there is the hardest part of the process. We all fear rejection and disappointment, so we decide to wait until next week, next month, or until we lose that nagging cough. One can't possibly begin during the summer, we tell ourselves, and it wouldn't do us any good to try around the holiday season. Then another set of excuses appears. Sooner or later, we reach the point where we won't make a call or send an email because Mercury is in retrograde.

How do you break that cycle? Here is my advice, derived from decades of experience: *pile all the information in this book into a three-month job finding campaign.*

Three months is all it should take. In order to squeeze everything into that timeframe, though, you're going to have to work at it daily. It's going to be a grind, so I want you to block off the time on the calendar now. Plan a celebration on the 91st day. Invite people to the gala celebrating your new role. Ask your Board of Directors to be there. Go into the next 90 days with the fixed notion that you will give a speech to everyone at your party explaining all the details of your new job.

That might sound a bit over the top, but I really do want you to put real pressure on yourself. It's true that the next few months might feel like agony at times, but right now reaching out to new contacts is your most important job. It is literally the one thing you have to do every day. Hold your feet to the fire. Do so much outreach that the pain and hurt of the job search actually become pleasurable.

Once you have that mindset, remember that some of it actually *can* be enjoyable. Not only is it exciting to discover your true talents and ambitions, but you can also celebrate milestones along the way.

Have a party after you write your life history. Build a portrait of your Ideal Prospect and then take the morning off!

Put everything you have into three days of research around your prospecting methods. Do your market research, gather up half a dozen targets from observation, and rack your brain to create a Center of Influence list. Then, when you're done, take the afternoon off and get yourself one of those new aromatherapy massages.

Run your contact list by your board and get more names. Then, spend another day grinding adding to your list. Set up those first

CI meetings. When you have a total of seven buy yourself a small present.

It's going to take a lot of work to become a prospecting expert and zero in on your 20 Ideal Prospects. As soon as you find them, and set up those meetings, I want you to take the whole weekend off and pamper yourself with whatever luxury or pastime brings you joy.

And finally, work like a mad person meeting with all those Ideal Prospects, writing handwritten thank-you notes, meeting fresh Centers of Influence, developing *more* Ideal Prospects, and generating job offers. When it's all done, and you're comparing one against another on your prioritized scorecard, you will be ready for the biggest sense of relief of all – knowing that your career is fully on track.

Now it's *really* time to celebrate!

Three months, spent wisely, is plenty of time to make all of this happen. But, I need you to be focused and locked in. So buckle up and get ready for bit of hard work.

Also, don't leave just yet. There are a few more tidbits of advice I want to give you before you start buying champagne for yourself and your Board of Directors... including what to do if you're afraid to get started or if it seems to be taking you longer than you thought to gain any traction.

24

GRAB YOUR COMPASS AND GET IN THE RIVER

I want you to imagine yourself as an explorer in another time. After weeks of traveling you find yourself perched on the top of the hill at the end of the known world. In the valley below lies a river that branches off into several different directions.

Picture a fast-moving current. When you look downstream you can see that there is a sharp bend in about half a mile. You know from consulting a map that this is a long and winding river with many different tributaries. You have also heard there are some rapids, but they aren't marked on your guide.

Your career is like that long, winding river. It's up to you to make your best guess about which direction to take. Then you have to jump in your canoe and get going. The current will provide all the momentum you need.

Some young people become very nervous at the prospect of diving in without knowing where they are going. That's understandable, but it's the only way. You can't fill in more of the map without exploring. As you move, new places and situations will be revealed to you. Some will be unexpected and maybe even unpleasant. That might be difficult, but at least you're *moving*.

Will you set off toward the rapids and rocks sometimes? Absolutely. But like any explorer, you'll carry a map and a compass. Whenever you find yourself in a situation that doesn't look or feel right you can retrace your steps and move off in a different direction. You'll fail – a little or a lot – and then make a new attempt with better information.

If that all sounds scary and uncertain then congratulate yourself on being alive. Then talk to someone (maybe on your own personal Board of Directors) who has enjoyed a successful career. They will likely tell you that their professional path wasn't a straight line from the bottom to the top. Most of us suffer through a lot of twists, turns, and setbacks... and you will, too.

So many young people are looking for the exact path that will lead them from the beginning of their career to the end. The uncertainty about what's to come, or even where they should start, keeps them from jumping into the boat at all. They think they are staying "safe," when in reality they are simply stuck in place.

It goes without saying that I don't want you to be foolhardy and rush into a course of action that's going to leave you in a bad spot. We need to pace ourselves, especially when moving through turns and twists and unknown waters. But in the end, we *do* have to get into the river and go with the current. Otherwise we can never move forward.

The job and career path you dream of are out there, but that doesn't mean you can find them without being willing to try new things.

What if It's Not Working?

Bringing this river analogy into today's world, you may be reading this book while sitting on the shore. Maybe you have not ventured into the river at all. Perhaps you have dipped your toes in the water but haven't really gotten wet. Now is the time to jump in.

What awaits you is a 40-year career marathon canoe trip. This stokes some level of fear in all of us because it seems such an uncertain voyage. That fear can immobilize us. Regardless of how good a fit that first job is, or maybe *isn't*, at least you jumped in your canoe and started paddling.

The need to start moving forward is why I want you to limit your search to three months. The imperative here is to get your trip started. Going back a bit in the book, the NFs of the world (like me) love adventure and have to worry about causing a shipwreck by going too fast. The NTs might fall in love with work on shore, exploring all the various and intricate models of what their trip might entail. The SJs are fearful of starting their trips at all, and might be tempted to shove off in their canoes while grabbing hold of tree limbs for safety. One only has to think back to the movie *What About Bob*, with the timid hero screaming "I'm sailing!" at his shrink. And last, the SPs will probably not have read this far into the book. Still, they will see a canoe, impulsively leap into it and start paddling with no final destination in mind. They just love the zest of living on the edge!

Regardless of which group you fall into, let's talk about the destination for a moment. Each one of us should have a goal of not only getting away from the shore, but also going as far as our God-given skills can carry us. The Latin phrase "cui suique," meaning "to each their own," might fit here. We are always moving forward, doing the very best we can. Each of us is unique and our definition of success can and should be very different than the other canoeists'.

Your journey won't be easy. You will run across rain, snow, sleet, and a host of other challenges. Things you never could have dreamed of will happen to you as you are paddling. One major Timbo commandment, though, is to bring your journal along for the ride. The process of discovering *Who am I?*, *What do I want?*, and *How do I get it?* doesn't end when you land that first job. Please remember this. Your journey has just started because you have many discoveries still to make.

The four deaths that occurred near me in the early '80s essentially sank my canoe for a while. I just lay down on the banks of the river and moaned, "Woe is me!" Finally, I picked myself up and realized those four men I had lost from my life would have kicked my ass if I just stayed there feeling sorry for myself. I literally heard their voices as they implored me to drive forward for their sakes if not mine. Lord, that got me back in the water and rowing faster than ever.

Every life has challenges. Some of these will directly affect your career. Others will change who you are on some level... which will also affect your career. Those sorts of major shifts might feel far away for you. They usually do, right until the moment everything changes.

Let's zoom back in on Haley and see how she did when her canoe was scuttled shortly after she took her second job.

Haley's Story

When the Covid-19 pandemic hit, the enjoyable parts of my job were all placed on pause. There weren't gatherings or live training events anymore. Everything had to be done from home or in a virtual meeting. That wasn't my employer's fault, of course, but it allowed me to view the position differently. That's when I discovered something interesting: when you took away the superficial perks, it wasn't really the opportu-

nity I had thought it was. There wasn't a great deal of room for advancement and the culture wasn't a perfect fit for my personality. Whereas my first job had probably leaned too heavily into the "work hard, play hard" ethos, my new bosses were incredibly laid back. It was no problem if I wanted to work from home half the week, for example, or show up late and leave early. I was craving more structure. I wanted to be surrounded by other competitors like me.

Instead of going into all the details I will just say I realized the specific job wasn't going to take me where I wanted to go and the culture wasn't a good match for my fiery personality. Suddenly, the crisis I had felt in the summer returned with a vengeance. I had only been in my new position for a few months. If I was worried about being a job hopper before, then I definitely had to think about the way another switch would look on my resume now. And besides, who would hire me if my track record made it look like I couldn't stick to any one company or direction?

I might have gotten confused or overwhelmed at this point except that I already had the tools I needed to deal with the situation. Rather than freaking out about the mess I found myself in, I decided to look at things objectively. I made a scorecard for my second job, just like I had the first one. I went beyond the kinds of pros and cons lists people make and thought seriously about where my discomfort was coming from. There were a lot of things I loved about the new opportunity I had, but also several warning signs I had ignored. I made the mistake of looking at the shiny and fun things in front of me rather than looking at the longer-term trajectory of my career.

In a weird way, the fact that I had made a mistake actually seemed like a good thing. I knew I could learn from it and avoid falling into the same trap again.

Although Tim and I had kept in touch in the six months since our meeting, I decided to reach out again and let him know what was happening. This time we didn't walk through a series of exercises. He just listened while I applied the lessons he had taught me to a new challenge. I already had the answers I was looking for. He just listened and gave me the space to figure that out.

What I ultimately came to were a pair of conclusions. The first one was that I didn't want to seem like someone who was hopping from one job to another and was afraid to admit I had made a big mistake. The second conclusion was that those things didn't matter. I just had to be brave, trust myself, and be willing to take a chance. If I wasn't going to be engaged in my work on a day-to-day basis then what was the point?

When I jumped into the job search process again it was with an even sharper sense of direction and purpose. I knew what I was looking for and how to go about searching for it. I reached out to my network, made introductions through LinkedIn, and even probed my alumni contacts. I didn't feel stressed about the process and didn't fall for the myth that there was one single opportunity that would be perfect. I knew there would be choices, trade-offs, and priorities to consider.

In the end, what felt like a big leap turned into an easy decision. It turned out my first boss, the one who knew my strengths and was a good match for my style, was starting her own firm. After leaving the company where I interned and started my career, she was striking out on her own and needed someone with my background.

The opening seemed like the perfect opportunity, but I knew it was more than just a happy coincidence. I had learned enough about myself through Tim's process to understand the role was a good match. It would require a lot of work and some crunch-time projects, but also give me the recognition and advancement opportunities I craved. My next job wasn't going to be in a glamorous office or with a worldwide company, but it would give me the chance to restart my career with a business that was growing by leaps and bounds. Haley, Inc. was back on track.

I would say I found my happy ending except Tim has taught me that no such thing exists. I can be happy, but this part of my story isn't an ending. I'll have to keep managing my career as I move forward, hopefully getting a little smarter and sharper along the way.

If you are anything like me you are probably figuring your life and career out one step at a time. You might not have all the answers you wish you did. Maybe you feel like you don't have the time to write a life history or think about whether you would be an astronaut or princess if someone gave you the choice.

What I can tell you is that going through Tim's exercises step by step made all the difference for me. I learned things about myself that seemed hidden right up until a eureka moment arrived. But the work doesn't finish itself. None of the exercises we went through together would have made a difference if I didn't buy into them. I was just lucky that Tim made it fun and doesn't take himself too seriously.

If you don't know what you want then you're never going to get it. Once I figured out the piece of the puzzle about my own strengths and values everything else fell into line. I bet it will for you, too. Good luck!

THE VIEW FROM THE OTHER SIDE

I f you are reading this final chapter then I'm going to assume you have followed my advice, found the kind of job you were looking for, and have begun positioning yourself toward a future that makes you feel excited and fulfilled.

You may have reached the end of your job search, at least for now, but there is still a lot of road ahead of you. You may find you will be looking for a new position sooner than expected, just as Haley did. Or you might discover that your needs and priorities change over time. You might even be so good at your job that you end up being recruited to another position within your own company, or another business, in the next few years.

How prepared you are for those possibilities will determine whether you are able to stay on a course that leads you toward happiness. This is where it helps to get advice from someone like your good friend Timbo who has been around long enough to see it all from a few different angles. Here are some final tips I want you to remember as time rolls on...

Embrace the Journey

You may have noticed I referred to your career as a journey. For most of us, that ends up being a pretty accurate description of things. I had no idea, back when I took my first teaching job, that I would end up running my own business as a coach decades later. Not only was the idea not on my radar, but such a job didn't even exist back then. Some of you who are reading these words will eventually work in positions and industries that are barely around today, or that haven't even been dreamed up yet.

That can be a scary thought, but you shouldn't let it frighten you. It's always the case that certain types of businesses and career paths are opening up and closing down. The more flexible you remain in your thinking, the easier it will be for you to ride the waves of change that are always coming over the horizon. It's also a lot less stressful to roll with the times than it is to freak out about every new technology or idea.

Even if you don't end up in a cutting-edge field there are probably going to be unexpected twists and turns in your working life. Very few life plans ever come to fruition as expected. Circumstances change, as do our desires. Learning about yourself, your talents, and your personality type puts you miles ahead of your friends and colleagues who have never followed the path of self-discovery. But that process never really finishes. You will still be learning about new aspects of your own mind decades from now. And as you do, you will be drawn to fresh challenges.

One good way to make sense of your thoughts and to process them more clearly it is to continue to keep some kind of journal. This doesn't have to be a document you add to every day, but it should be a place where you can store notes, thoughts, and impressions every week or so.

Another reason to journal through your life and career journey is that it can help you in times of stress. You might have particularly strong feelings, or even breakthrough moments of clarity when you are in the midst of stress or euphoria. A few months later, though, your memories of those events will have faded. By writing things down you leave yourself a record you can return to later. So, if ever you are wondering how you got through an experience, or what you could have learned from it, there will be notes to return to.

And finally, your journal itself could have value at some point. I waited decades to finally start writing the books I knew were inside of me. As I began the process of unpacking my emotions and experiences with an editor, the written records I shared and reviewed kept me honest. I could choose what to include or take away from my story, but I could always remember the struggles or emotions I was dealing with at various stages in my life because they were put into words right in front of me.

Keep Running *MyCo*

Speaking of the changes that happen over time, it's important to keep running *MyCo* like the business it is. Although it's a mental framework to understand your career instead of a literal company, I hope you'll come back to the CEO mindset behind it on a regular basis.

Companies assess their performance regularly. As CEO you should be checking in at least once a year. Some years are going to call for champagne. Others might require you to take a deeper look into your books to see where you have gone wrong. That's just the nature of life and business, and all the good and bad outcomes give you more data to work with. This review gives you the opportunity to think about your next "one-year plan" based on all of the new facts that have come to light.

The idea here isn't that you're going to start looking for a new job or challenge every year. Instead, it's to prevent an all-too-common phenomenon where people in their 30s, 40s, and 50s suddenly find themselves adrift. I meet these men and women all the time, and most feel like they just woke up one day with no idea about how they inherited the lives and careers they are living through. They have a sense of being frustrated and disoriented all at the same time.

Most of the time, the problems these folks are facing can be traced back to the fact that they have never gone through the sorts of exercises I have recommended to you. They picked a job, and then another two, or two dozen, after that, based on a whim (or more likely, financial gain). Then they ended up somewhere they didn't necessarily want to be because it was the path of least resistance.

However, even if you start off in the right direction it is easy to end up far off course. Even if you don't change, your company and industry will. That's why it's so valuable for you to check in with yourself from time to time to make sure you like the life and career you seem to be working toward.

MyCo will keep functioning as a single-person entity whether you take leadership of it or not. Given that you have to do all the work for your business – and be satisfied with the paycheck and benefits it provides – shouldn't you be the one in charge of the direction it takes?

Don't Fire Your Board of Directors

Time for a quick but important reminder. Just as *MyCo* still needs to be monitored even after you find a new job, your Board of Directors has value even when you aren't looking to change things up.

This isn't to say you'll speak to these people about your career every month, or even every year. But you chose them because they have perspectives you don't, along with a vested interest in helping you be successful. It's never a bad idea to keep individuals like that plugged into your life, particularly when you're thinking about making big professional decisions.

As your goals, priorities, and circumstances change, so too might your board. Some people might drift out of your life, just as new mentors will appear. You might rely less on former professors, as an example, and more on senior managers within your industry or organization. Some of your board members might pass away or lose interest; you might incorporate the advice of a new father-in-law or department head to replace them.

What matters here is not that you maintain the same set of individuals within your inner circle of advisors, but that you have people you know and trust giving you advice when you need it most. No matter how far you go, or how high you climb, you'll want those voices to count.

One more thing you might want to consider is being on another person's Board of Directors. It may take a long time before you feel like you know what you are doing in your career. But I want you to remember that things seem a lot different to someone who is just a year or two behind you on the same path. They don't have the knowledge and experience you do. If you get the chance to help another person on their journey, take it. It feels good. It also gives you a chance to reflect on what you have learned and see your career in a different light.

Set Bigger and Better Goals

Now that we're coming toward the end of the book, it's time for me to share the biggest and most important truth of all. What I have taught you in these chapters isn't just how to find a job or take control of your career, but a formula you can use to improve your life again and again.

That might sound like a big claim, but let's take it in parts. First, I had you think about who you are and where you are at. Next, I asked you to clarify your desires and create a plan to move ahead. Then, you took action to achieve a certain result. And finally, you got a chance to review and recalibrate.

This is the same process you would follow if you wanted to become a homeowner, move to another part of the world, or start your own business. The specifics might change from one project or goal to the next, but the overall formula would remain the same.

I often explain my model of personal change in very simple terms. First, I asked my coaching client to imagine a frog sitting on a lily pad. Then, I have them envision that this frog wants to reach another lily pad that is too far away to reach by jumping. What do they have to do to make it to their destination? The answer, of course, is to find one or two lily pads in the middle. Once the path and destination are clear, the way forward is obvious.

Whenever you feel stuck in life, consider that the solution is likely hiding from you for one of two reasons. It's either the case that you don't know what your destination looks like or that you aren't sure how to reach it. Those are really the only two conclusions. And both answers are easier to find when you understand who you are and where you are at.

The lily pad image might seem like a simple way to approach your life or the world around you, but it works. I have taught this analogy to new and recent graduates like yourself, and to executives and entrepreneurs who are worth millions and millions of dollars. No matter who you are or what phase of your life you have reached, it can be easy to lose track of what really matters. There are constant disruptions that keep us from seeing things clearly. But once we get back to our roots, and the basics, there is always the chance to set off in a new direction.

Don't Be Afraid to Surprise Yourself

I'll conclude this, my first published book, with an ending that is a big surprise to me! Even though I have clearly finished my own personal 40-year marathon and my career "canoe" is stored away in dry dock, writing this book has helped me believe I need to get back to those rapids one more time. Why? I believe I have accomplished the goal I began with, which was to help you as a young person launch your boat and land that first tide to what you truly want. What hit me in the process, however, is that even though what I've given you should be incredibly helpful now, it won't be enough to prepare you for the changes that will come farther down the river.

Ponder this: although I believed I was barely hanging on at the beginning of my career, the biggest rapids I faced in my canoe were yet to even arrive. It wasn't until my 30s and 40s that my more significant challenges were to come. I've seen the same in literally thousands of coaching clients. Things may get harder as you go. Having the right sense of direction can spare you some of the stress and headaches, but sooner or later you're going to face some issues that are outside the scope of this book.

With that in mind, I have concluded I really have to write the sequel to this first title. In this book, our central focus has been on getting your career off to a good start. That's important. But eventually you'll discover the same thing I did during my own personal journey: that work life is never truly separate from the other parts of life.

These other pieces need to be integrated into your work life. This "Whole You" or "Whole Me" contains aspects like:

1.Family – both original and present

2.Marriage or love life

3.Spiritual life

4.Avocations like piano, journalism, pottery, etc.

5.Leisure time activities such as sports, exercise, socializing, old friends, reading, etc.

The realization that each of you will eventually need to know how to put it all together never hit me until I began to ask myself how I wanted to end this book. That's when it dawned on me that I should write my second book on how to find balance, peace and, yes, happiness.

It took writing a whole book for me to figure out I have more work to do. So, the river continues to move me along and I just keep paddling. It means there is a lot still to come, but as you'll find it's a lot more fun to steer through the unexpected twists and turns than it is to sit on the shore. I never saw this adventure coming, but I hope you'll join me for the ride!

APPENDIX

On the following pages you will find sample job search scorecards and introduction letters. Feel free to adapt them to your own use as needed.

Sample Scorecard

	Most Imp.	Opportunity 1	Opportunity 2	Opportunity 3
Money	*			
Support Mechanisms	*			
Geography				
Mentor	*			
Growth	*			
Learning	*			
Pace	*			
Exciting				
Quality of Company	*			
Quality of Associates				
Title				
3 to 5 year "Dream"				
Feel Calm				
Being a Resource				
Supportive Environment				
Network Building				
Independence				
Vacations				
Benefits				
Close to Career Planning	*			
Loosey Goosey				
Definable Job				
A "Cause"				
Chance to write/do other things				
Lego Exercise				
Make Presentations				
Creative				
Feel Needed and Wanted				
Associated with Class				
Prestige				

Additional Sample Scorecard

	THE JOB	Opportunity 1	Opportunity 2	Opportunity 3
1.	THE JOB			
	Overtime			
	Best Bridge Job			
	Apprenticeship			
	Use personal & technical skills			
	Balance with home and work			
	Value added			
	See projects through to end			
	Goal-driven job			
	Some travel			
	Involved in day-to-day decisions			
	Money			
	Geography			
	No weekends			
	Not pulled 10 different ways			
2.	THE COMPANY			
	Rapport			
	Talented and ambitious people			
	Aggressive			
	Basic industry but interesting			
	Growing			
	Friendly			
3.	MY BOSS			
	Priorities of life are straight			
	Technical			
	Well-rounded			
	Personable			
	Knows how to flatter me			
	Cuts through issues quickly			
	Not a user			
4.	CHEMISTRY			
	Quality of life			
	Well-rounded			
	Relaxed, feels comfortable			
	Flexible environment, yoga)			
	Feel wanted and respected			
	Regular folks			
5.	ME			
	Odds beater			
	Flattery			
	Time to self			
	Feels prestigious			
	Sarcasm, cynicism fits in			

Sample Letter to a Referred Lead from a Center of Influence

Dear Mr./Ms. [name]:

Recently, Tom Smith suggested that I be in touch with you. Let me explain. Tom has been a good friend for years and I recently asked him for some suggestions on my job search.

I am a recent graduate of Boston College and was a business major. My approach to the job market is, I think, fairly unique. Being a hockey player my whole life and quite competitive, I decided that I needed an edge over all the other recent graduates. So, I built a model of what I wanted in my first and subsequent jobs. Quite specific, I might add. When I sat down with Tom, I took him through this picture of my Ideal Job. He was quite impressed and gave me three names to call on. You were one of those three. Tom told me to stress in these three meetings the rather unusual summer jobs and internships which I have experienced.

My hope would be to meet you for 30 minutes or so to hear more about you and your organization. I now have 17 names to call on from my visits with people like Tom Smith. By not focusing on only "known" jobs, my belief is that a real job will appear from these many meetings. At the very least, I would hope that you could replace yourself with another referral following our brief meeting. Thanks in advance for meeting with me

Sincerely,

Sample Letter to Target with no Referral

Dear Mr./Ms. [name, title, etc.]:

I recently read the Executive Profile of you in the Boston Globe. It was excellent. I especially liked your honest story of how difficult it was for you to land your first job after college. While it is true that this is a cold letter, could you spare me 30 minutes as I launch my own career as a recent college graduate? Let me explain.

I believe that I took a fairly creative approach to my search. In essence, I built a very clear model of the Ideal Job based on who I am, what I have done and what I want. It was almost eerie when I read the article about you- almost a complete match of what I want. In short, I wanted a top-notch sales training program just like the one you started at your firm. I also wanted a company with genuine Midwestern values - your Nebraska roots qualified!

I would love to visit and learn more about your company and share my career model with you. At the very least, my hopes would be that you could give me a few ideas or even prospects to call on. Thanks for the opportunity to meet with you.

Sincerely,

ACKNOWLEDGMENTS

I struggle with authors who take several pages to thank all the people behind the scenes who helped the writer. On the other hand, this is my first book, so please cut me a little slack as I do the same!

First, I thank Ma and Dad. Ma for her rich lyrical background and for her love of both me and the classics. I majored in Latin due to her, as did my sisters. She gave me a deep and wacky imagination, creativity and an affinity for the beauty of words and word pictures. To Dad, my thanks for giving me a belief in hard work as well as the magnetic pull of humor.

I thank my wife, Maryann, for her belief in me and my writing. She became the coach of the coach! It's a beautiful thing that, despite all the yelling at each other tied to the endless hours of editing and my being a picayune editor who drove her nuts, we came out the far end with the same beautiful relationship. And special thanks to my four children (Lisa, Kelly, JT III and Meredith) for allowing me to act as their dad, a role that I loved and treasured through all these decades.

To my readers: please pay close attention to how all these career "layers" happened. One tier led to the next. I never could have imagined any of this before the voyage started. You have read a lot about getting your career canoe out in the current and moving downstream, as then more things reveal themselves. Thus did it happen to me.

The first building block was my 10-year consulting gig with Arthur Andersen & Co. Dan Archabal, a high school friend, referred me to his boss Bill Meagher somewhere around 1981. Bill ran the Boston office of Arthur Andersen & Co. You read about this in Chapter Two, titled *The Tale of Timbo*. Andersen was one of the "Big 8" audit, tax, and systems consulting firms. My career strategic plan laid out a desire to be a career development teacher. Thanks, deeply, guys for taking that risk on me now some 40 years later! Nine long years of working deeply with Arthur Andersen and their clients as a consultant paved the way for me creating my own firm in 1990.

The next building block was my 10-year stretch of consulting in the 1990s to Dr. Art Russo, who was the newly named CEO of the clinical system at UMass Medical School. Ten years of consulting with Art, his senior team, and the 18 or so chairs gave me valuable experience in the healthcare field, which turned out to be the perfect world for me to live in for the next 30 years. Thank you, Art, and I'm grateful to have you and your family as good friends to this day.

Next, I thank Peter Markell, the recently retired chief administrative officer of Partners Healthcare (since re-branded as Mass General Brigham). Arthur Andersen was a 10-year gig and UMass Worcester another 10, meaning Peter and I have worked together for over 20 years while sharing a deep commitment to providing excellent customer service – Peter to all his internal customers and me to Peter. Relationships of trust have been the hallmark of the work of Wellesley Partners, my consulting company.

The next important origin of this book ran concurrently during the 2000s with Stephen Hardy, who was a Bowdoin hockey teammate. Oh, the fun we had together at Bowdoin pretending to be adults! Steve was a classics major with me and he went on to receive a PhD in the history of sport. Steve is now a retired professor from the kinesiology department at the University of New Hampshire. The roots of this book are most clearly linked to Steve inviting me to speak to his senior majors about their future careers. When Steve told me that the material was incredibly helpful to his students, he planted the idea for this book in my head. Steve is, by the way, a real scholar while I remain a half-assed scholar. He is also a brilliant researcher; I just didn't have the patience. Steve is the co-author of a fantastic book (more like a tome) called *Hockey, A Global History*.

Thanks also to another Bowdoin hockey teammate, Dr. Robert McGuirk, who was my freshman roommate. We have reconnected over the past few years, which has been wonderful. Rob became a fan of my material and gave me so much help, support, and guidance back when I was really stuck on how to organize all my material. It meant a lot to me and really helped. Thanks, Rob!

Lastly, a very special word of thanks to my editor, Matt, for helping me get the words just right. Thanks, Matt!

ABOUT THE AUTHOR

Tim Sullivan is an executive coach, entrepreneur, and first-time author. Although he has 30+ years of experience working with physician executives, he began his career as a teacher and hockey coach. Even as his career evolved he never lost his passion for helping young people find their best career paths.

When he's not coaching or writing, Tim lives with his wife, Maryann, on the south coast of Massachusetts. He has four children and eight grandchildren who remain the pride and joy of his life.

Made in the USA
Columbia, SC
03 December 2021

50335578R00112